OF THE MAGIC VALLEY

MYCHEL MATTHEWS

TIMES-NEWS
PUBLICATIONS

Copyright © 2015 Times-News.

All rights reserved.

ISBN: 1517208947
ISBN 13: 9781517208943

DEDICATION

To the Twin Falls County Historical Museum, which captured my heart just six years ago and continues to inspire me.

—M.M.

Table of Contents

PAGE

1	Shoshone Falls Hotel Burns
1	Harriman's Alaska Expedition Visits Shoshone Falls
2	Rock Creek Jim
4	The Worst Single Slaughter of American Indians
5	Ezra Meeker, Father of the Oregon Trail
6	W.H. Baugh, Shoshone Doctor, Builder
7	The Steam-engine Tractor in the Snake River
9	The Mummy of John Wilkes Booth
10	Early Immigrant Jimmy Yamamoto
11	DeWitt Young, Early Fireman and County Commissioner
12	Marsh Basin, Early Seat of Cassia County
13	The Pony Express (Sort of) Came through Here
14	Shoshone Ice Cave
15	Monsters of the River
16	Frank Gooding: Why Magic Valley is in Mountain Time Zone
17	The Mormon Trail
18	Twin Falls County's 1st Elected Sheriff
19	Remnants of Peavey's Whistle Stop
20	Execution or Lynching?
21	Stagecoaches in the Magic Valley
22	I.B. Perrine's 'Town House'
22	Hollister, a 'New' Municipality

PAGE	
23	The Minidoka Relocation Center
25	The Twin Falls American Legion Hall
25	Opera in Twin Falls
27	The Bucket of Blood Saloon
29	Photographer Charles R. Savage
29	Death Valley Scotty
31	The Shoshone Falls Bridge
32	The Methodist Church on Shoshone Street
34	Tom Bell's Long Plunge
35	Anna Daly, Buhl's First Elected Woman School Trustee
37	A Few Words from the Buhl School Superintendent
38	Fighting Fires in Twin Falls
39	Hailey, Seat of 2 Counties
40	The Riverside Inn at Milner
41	Magic Valley's Founding Fathers
43	Mining on the Snake River
44	The Home of Robert and Alice McCollum, Social Center
45	The Robert McCollum House Mix-up
46	Twin Falls' 1st Christmas Celebration
47	Twin Falls County Poor Farm
48	Twin Falls' First Jail
49	B-24 Crash on Mount Harrison
50	Location of Twin Falls Train Depot Carefully Contemplated
51	Addison T. Smith
53	Twin Falls Golf Club

PAGE	
54	Fair Times
55	The Day the River Went dry
55	'Ee Dah How' Not the Origin of Idaho
56	The Albion Normal School: Training Students to be Teachers
57	Roseworth: A Failed Settlement
58	Al Faussett Shoots the Falls
60	Early Twin Falls a Lonely Place
61	John Hansen, Busy Pioneer
63	Nat-Soo-Pah Becomes a Tourist Attraction
63	Jack Rabbits, Scourge of the Past
64	Barrymore: Almost a Town
65	May Day, a Celebration
66	The Need for Speed
67	Farm Labor Camps in WWII
68	Horse Thieves and Escaped Bears at Devils Corral
69	Harmon Park: a Gift to the Community
70	The Rise of Moving Pictures in Twin Falls
71	The Rogerson Hotel was Early Elegance in Twin Falls
73	Remember the Maine
74	Idaho's 3 Capitols and 2 Capitals
75	Fugitive Evades the Hangman's Noose
76	When Blue Lakes Boulevard Met the Perrine Waterfall
78	A 'Merrie' Christmas from Twin Falls Photographers
79	Winter of 1948-49 Was Beautiful and Treacherous
81	I.B. Perrine vs. the Beaver

PAGE	
82	Bisbee's Wife was his Muse
83	The City of Rocks Stage Station
85	Lind Automobile Co.: 1st Car Dealership in Twin Falls
85	A Story of Family at Callen Corner
87	Wilbur Hubbell: Buhl's National League Hero
88	Fighting Alcohol before Prohibition
89	Air Force Jet, Car Collision on U.S. 93
91	Before the Cottage Motel Fell Apart
92	Tom Blodgett: Minister with a Controversial Side
93	The Great Dinosaur Caper of 1963
96	Some Dreams are too Big
97	The KKK in the Magic Valley
98	The Turf Club Has Been Here and There
100	Making Hay when the Sun Shines
101	Vegas Vic Continues to Wave in Twin Falls
102	A New Search for an Old School Pool
103	A Grand View
104	The Most American Thing in America
104	Your Guess is as Good as Mine
105	Shoshone Falls: An Unfulfilled Memorial
106	Long Defunct Towns in Twin Falls County
108	Bisbee's Sense of Humor Showed a Soft Spot for Bunnies
108	There's Magic in this Valley
109	Henry Harris: the Legendary Black Buckaroo
110	Sleuth Finds Pistol Likely Used in Century Old Murders

PAGE	
112	The Staircase at Kiwanis Nook
114	Headstones are all that Remain of Artesian City
116	The Wizard of Kimberly Road
118	Buildings Lost over the Years
120	The Tragic Tale of Lew and Ella Newton
121	Early Landowners Weren't Always Homesteaders
123	Happy Holly Brings Big Names to Town
125	Charlie McMaster's Horses
126	A Snapshot of the Idaho Territory
128	'Owyhee' Means Hawaii
129	How the Malad River Got Its Name
130	Was Dowdle Bill Really a Scoundrel?
132	Canal Water Was Used for More than Irrigation
133	Not-so-funny Money
135	The Power Plant at Shoshone Falls
136	The Mormon Corridor in Idaho
137	Bisbee's Muse Arrives in Twin Falls
138	The Legacy of Harry Barry
140	Appearance is Everything
141	The Town of Rock Creek
142	Safe Roads for Washington School
144	Bringing Serial Killer Lyda Southard to Justice
146	The Conviction and Escape of Lyda Southard
148	The White Elephant in the City Park
150	Mike's Cabin Burns in Cave Canyon Fire
151	The Perrine Monuments at Bryan Point
153	Mosler Safe at the Twin Falls County Courthouse

FOREWORD

It's no secret to anyone in southern Idaho that I.B. Perrine founded the Twin Falls Land and Water Co. in 1900, transforming the sagebrush desert into an agricultural oasis that gave birth to the communities that now make up what we call the Magic Valley.

Local historians thoroughly documented the important dates, names and events that followed over the next century.

This book's author, Mychel Matthews, is a fine historian in her own right. A former director of the Twin Falls County Historical Museum and chairwoman of the Twin Falls County Historic Preservation Commission, she's one of the most knowledgeable experts on southern Idaho.

She's also a fine journalist.

Matthews plays both roles as the writer of the Times-News' weekly "Hidden History" column, which showcases the colorful characters and lesser-known stories from our region's history. In her column, many of the names and places might be familiar to readers, but their behind-the-scenes stories seldom are.

It's the secret to her column's popularity. Historians document history; journalists bring it to life. Matthews does both.

Each column and photograph in this volume was originally published as a "Hidden History" column in the Times-News. Matthews selected her favorites for this book.

She's quick to credit the historians who provided her source material. But I'd be remiss if I didn't highlight Matthews' dogged work to dig deeper into each person, place and event for the hidden details that make her columns sing.

It's been my pleasure to edit many of these columns. I find even deeper joy reading them. I hope you do, too.

Matt Christensen
Editor, Times-News

PREFACE

The problem with history is that it happened a long time ago.
Resources and details are lost over time.
Stories change and memories fade.
And "facts" often vary from the get-go.

In my "Hidden History" columns, I heavily relied on various photographers' documentation of the Magic Valley's past. I chose many of Twin Falls photographer Clarence E. Bisbee's images to illustrate the stories you will read in this book.

But many of the Bisbee photos lack specific details—Bisbee seldom labeled his photos and, when he did, he sometimes labeled them inaccurately. My job—not as a historian, but as a storyteller—is to weave a thread through all possible versions of the past to come up with a story that makes the most sense.

In this book, I offer you a taste of Magic Valley history—and I hope it whets your appetite for more.

Mychel Matthews

Shoshone Falls Hotel Burns

The hotel at Shoshone Falls, a once-grand building that had fallen into disrepair, burned to the ground in 1915.

The two-story landmark, built in 1886, offered 22 guest rooms, outhouses and a splendid view of the falls. The hotel and land on the south side of the falls was owned by W.A. Clark, a senator from Montana.

After 30 years, the hotel had deteriorated to the point that management no longer rented its rooms. It was said that the hotel was being used for gambling and prostitution.

PHOTO COURTESY OF TWIN FALLS COUNTY HISTORICAL SOCIETY
The hotel at Shoshone Falls was built in 1886 by W.A. Clark, a senator from Montana. Clark also owned that land surrounding the falls. In 1915, the hotel was destroyed by fire.

A dance was held the evening of Aug. 11 at John B. White's pavilion next to the hotel. The fire was discovered in the wee hours of the next morning by the man who ran the Shoshone Falls ferry.

Twin Falls resident Ed Dufresne was asleep in the hotel and had to be roused by the ferry master, the *Twin Falls Weekly Times* reported.

Authorities presumed that a smoldering cigar started the fire, amid rumors that prominent women from Twin Falls burned down the house of ill repute.

Harriman's Alaska Expedition Visits Shoshone Falls

PHOTO COURTESY OF CHARLES R. SAVAGE, BRIGHAM YOUNG UNIVERSITY LIBRARY
One of I.B. Perrines' stagecoaches is seen in this early C.R. Savage photograph.

Even before the town of Twin Falls was founded, many noted personalities visited the valley. In May 1899, E.H. Harriman, then the executive committee chairman of the Union Pacific Railroad, and more than 100 of the country's best scientists, photographers, artists, writers and naturalists visited Shoshone Falls and the Snake River Canyon.

Harriman, 51 at the time, was one of the most powerful men in America. But by the late 19th century, he was worn out and his doctor told him to take a vacation. Harriman decided to go to Alaska to hunt Kodiak bears.

HIDDEN HISTORY

He wouldn't go alone; Harriman gathered a scientific community to explore the coast of Alaska with him.

He told Clinton Hart Merriam, head of the Division of Economic Ornithology and Mammalogy at the U.S. Department of Agriculture and a founder of the National Geographic Society, that he would cover the group's expenses if Merriam would choose the guests.

The Harriman Alaska Expedition, a party of 126, explored coastlines from Seattle to Siberia and back again on the steamship "George W. Elder." The remodeled ship featured luxury rooms, a library, a stable for animals and taxidermy studios.

The guest list included Merriam, photographer Edward Curtis, ornithologist Charles Keeler, geographer Henry Gannett, botanist Thomas Kearney, naturalist John Muir, bird artist Louis Agassiz Fuertes and writer and conservationist John Burroughs.

Harriman took the expedition through Idaho by rail on the way to Seattle. A telegram reached the Shoshone depot just days before the special train arrived in town.

"Word was sent around to the whole countryside to be on hand early on the morning of (May 27) with all the conveyances available to take this group to see Shoshone Falls," H.J. Kingsbury, publisher of Kingsbury Printing Co., wrote in his book "Bucking the Tide."

Every buckboard, wagon, buggy and saddle horse — even one of I.B. Perrine's stagecoachs — showed up at the depot.

"When the train arrived, the greatest collection of nondescript vehicles ever assembled in a small Western town was on hand to meet them," Kingsbury said.

Rock Creek Jim

In the Twin Falls Cemetery lies a headstone that reveals little about the man commonly known as Rock Creek Jim.

Jim Lewis was a Shoshoni chief, born in the Duck Valley area only a dozen years after white explorers first came through the region. He lived out much of his life in the Magic Valley before Idaho became a state.

Jim said he was 100 years old just before the time of his death in September 1924, as his headstone attests, but there's no way to confirm or deny his claim.

Lulu Lough knew Jim and his family, and she recorded her childhood memories of him for Idaho's territorial centennial celebration in 1963.

Jim "grew tired of the way of the Indian," Lulu wrote, and tried most of his life "to emulate the white man's way of living."

MYCHEL MATTHEWS

MYCHEL MATTHEWS, TIMES-NEWS
Jim Lewis, better known as "Rock Creek Jim," is buried in the Twin Falls Cemetery. He died in 1924 at the age of 100. His headstone was donated by the Seventy Niners Assocation, a local group of old-timers.

He built a cabin at Rock Creek and lived there for years before moving to Whisky Slough, west of the Salmon Falls Creek.

When he became unhappy in his marriage, he burned down his cabin and left his wife behind, Lulu said. He rebuilt at Antelope Springs. The springs went dry after about a year, so he packed his horses and moved to the foothills in Cedar Creek Valley, built a cabin and furnished it with a table and chairs, a cook stove and a bed.

Jim traveled to Duck Valley and found an Indian woman called Susie. The couple had three children before Susie died.

After she died, Jim tore down his cabin and "turned it around so that evil spirits couldn't find the door," Lulu said.

"Jim was a good neighbor and always reassured us when rumors of Indian uprisings drifted in," she said.

Jim's sister, Mary, would weave willow baskets for Lulu's mother, and would take Lulu and her brother into the hills to dig what she called "joyic" bulbs. Mary taught the children how to eat red ants without getting bitten.

"They are as sour as the sourest pickle," she said.

As was custom, Jim's daughter Maggie, at 16, married the tribe's medicine man, an old man known as Jack.

Members of the tribe would visit Jim on their way home from fishing along the Wood River. On one trip, 40 Indians with some 75 paint horses camped near Lulu's home on Cedar Creek on their way to see their chief. Maggie and Jack accompanied the travelers.

Early the next morning, Lulu's uncle, John, heard a shot and when he investigated, he was told Jack had killed himself.

John found Jack's body with a string tied between his finger and the trigger, but there were no powder burns. Maggie had killed Jack, Lulu said.

Jim feared that Maggie would be killed in retaliation if she returned to Duck Valley, so he asked Lulu's father to take her in. Maggie lived with Lulu's family for a year before she remarried.

HIDDEN HISTORY

Jim gave the tribe "five steers and seven ponies each year to pay for the death of their medicine man," Lulu said.

Rock Creek Jim died at the old Twin Falls Hospital. Soon after, the Seventy Niners Association, a group of old-timers who came to the area before 1880, donated a simple headstone for his grave.

The Worst Single Slaughter of American Indians

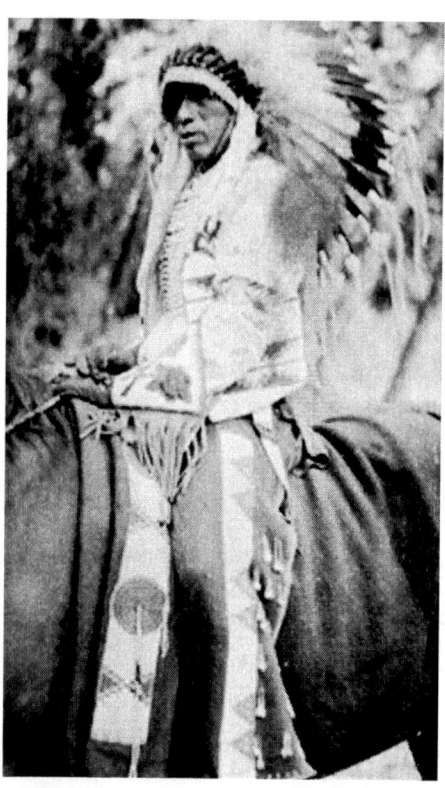

COURTESY PHOTO
A Northwestern Band Shoshoni warrior is seen in this undated photo.

Nearly 153 years ago, the worst single slaughter of American Indians in U.S. history occurred along the Bear River just north of the Utah border.

Franklin is the oldest permanent settlement in Idaho and was settled in 1860 by 13 Mormon families. The area was also the winter home of the Northwestern Band of the Shoshone Nation, led by Chief Sagwitch and War Chief Bear Hunter.

Friction between early settlers and the Shoshone developed and Utah Governor Frank Fuller asked the U.S. Secretary of War to provide a temporary regiment of mounted rangers to protect the settlers along the Utah-Idaho border.

Col. Patrick E. Connor — who was known for his belief that Indians were violent savages who needed to be destroyed at all costs — and his California Volunteers were ordered to Fort Douglas, Utah.

After an incident in which several settlers were killed, Connor sent a small infantry north from the fort with artillery and supply wagons. Four days later, Connor and his cavalry set out in deep snow and freezing temperatures to attack the winter camp the Shoshone called Boa Ogoi, 140 miles away.

As he left the fort, Connor promised to take no prisoners.

The group travelled at night to conceal their approach, but a white friend warned Sagwitch that Connor was coming in search of revenge.

Connor and 200 of his men arrived at the camp at 6 a.m. on Jan. 29, 1863. Sagwitch expected Connor, but the camp was not ready to do battle, said his granddaughter Mae Parry.

"He thought that perhaps this military man was a wise and just man," said Parry. "He thought the colonel would ask for the guilty men, whom he would immediately have handed over."

But Connor didn't ask any questions. His men began firing when the sun rose.

The Boa Ogoi camp sat in a protected ravine above the Bear River and was easily defended. But the well-armed military force was too much for the 400 or 500 Shoshoni.

Some jumped into the freezing river and drowned. Some swam to safety and joined other Shoshone bands.

But most — men, women and children — were killed.

Bear Hunter was tortured and eventually killed. Sagwitch escaped during the four-hour battle and survived.

A small number of children were spared and adopted by Mormon families.

In all, the Shoshone death toll is estimated at 350. Connor lost two dozen men.

Ezra Meeker, Father of the Oregon Trail

Ezra Meeker was 22 years old when he first passed through here. Meeker, along with his wife, Eliza Jane, and his infant son, Marion, followed the Old Oregon Trail west in 1852, in search of the American Dream.

Meeker settled in what would become Puyallup, Wash., where he amassed a fortune and became one of the most influential men in the state.

Hard times in the 1890s destroyed his financial empire, so Meeker started a new life devoted to preserving the Oregon Trail — the route that took more than 300,000 emigrants west.

The Oregon Trail was beginning to disappear across the West. The trail had been plowed under in many places and progress threatened to erase it from the nation's collective memory.

Determined to keep the historic pioneer trail from fading into obscurity, Meeker set out with a team of oxen and a covered wagon, and traveled back east over the route he had taken some 50 years before.

The attention Meeker drew to the Oregon Trail on his numerous trips across the West resulted in the eventual preservation of the trail and its alternate routes.

The white-haired, bearded pioneer caused a stir everywhere he went. He stopped at each town along the way and gave speeches about the

HIDDEN HISTORY

PHOTO COURTESY OF TWIN FALLS COUNTY HISTORICAL SOCIETY
C.E. Bisbee took this photo of Ezra Meeker, the father of the Oregon Trail, at Main Avenue and Shoshone Street in Twin Falls.

Oregon Trail. In 1910, on his second trip back, an 80-year-old Meeker spoke at Shoshone Falls to a large gathering celebrating Twin Falls County's first Flag Day.

Meeker charged a fee — 10 cents for adults and a nickel for children — to view his wagon, which was painted with slogans advertising the Oregon Trail.

In 1924, at the age of 94, Meeker flew from Vancouver, Wash., over the Oregon Trail to Dayton, Ohio, in an open-cockpit plane, piloted by Lt. Oakley Kelley. The next day, he rode in a parade with Orville Wright, then flew to Washington, D.C., to meet with President Calvin Coolidge.

In 1883, the Oregon Short Line railroad had made its way to town and with it came Meeker who gave the president his plan to designate a national highway honoring the Oregon Trail.

W.H. Baugh, Shoshone Doctor, Builder

Shoshone was once a rough and rowdy place — a true "Wild West" town. By 1883, the Oregon Short Line railroad had made its way to town and with it came new businesses that served nearby mines.

About 20 years later, Shoshone became the land port for construction materials that built other towns in the Magic Valley.

In 1911, Shoshone doctor W.H. Baugh built an opera house and hotel on Rail

Street. The building still stands. Dr. Baugh also owned property in Twin Falls — an empty lot on the north corner of Main Avenue and Shoshone Street, across the street from the modern Hotel Perrine.
In 1915, a newspaper article criticized Baugh for holding back progress in downtown Twin Falls. Only a small fruit orchard and fruit stand occupied the prime lot.
The doctor got to work and finished the Baugh building in 1916. The building was first occupied by Skeels-Wiley Drug Store, which was affiliated with Walgreen's. Later, Leonard Emerson ran the City Drug in the building for 30 years. It became Dunken's Draught House in 1990.

Dr. W.H. Baugh completed the Baugh building, on the north corner of Main Avenue and Shoshone Street in Twin Falls, after being criticized for holding back progress downtown.

The Steam-engine Tractor in the Snake River

If you float the Snake River when the water is low, you might get a glimpse of a steam-engine tractor lying on its side in the river east of the Perrine Memorial Bridge.
But the details of how the tractor came to rest in the canyon have been as murky as the river itself – until now.
Some say the steam engine was used to build the first rim-to-rim bridge, and was pushed off the bridge when the work was completed in 1927. Others say it was driven over the canyon rim when the state of Idaho purchased the bridge in 1940, to celebrate the end of the toll to cross the bridge.
As it turns out, the steam engine's dive into the river had nothing to do with the bridge at all.
"I remember it as clear as day," said George Paxton, whose father drove the machine to the edge of the canyon before it took the plunge. The event, Paxton said, was a publicity stunt to mark the end of the steam engine era.
Steam-engine tractors, which revolutionized farming in the late 19th century, operated much like the steam-engine locomotives of the day. Coal or wood was shoveled into a firebox under a boiler, heating water to create steam to power the machine's engine.
The tractors were finicky, difficult to maneuver and dangerous to operate. So when the internal combustion engine began to replace the steam engine,

DREW NASH, TIMES-NEWS
In 1911, Shoshone doctor W.H. Baugh built an opera house and hotel on Rail Street.

manufacturers of farm equipment were quick to embrace the new technology. In the early 1900s, small tractors that ran on fuel oil were developed for use on the farm. By World War II, steam-engine tractors were all but obsolete.

Paxton, 84, was about 10 years old when his father, John Paxton, and farm-equipment dealer Harley Williams, made plans to drive a steam engine over the canyon rim.

Williams, owner of Williams Tractor, had taken the steam-engine tractor in on trade for a new Case tractor.

Williams and the elder Paxton were good friends. Paxton was an expert operator of the steam-engine tractor — and Williams needed someone who could drive the tractor to the canyon rim, without going over the rim with it. The year, to the best of the younger Paxton's recollection, was about 1938. A large group of partiers gathered on the north side of the canyon, upstream from the bridge.

"It was a big promotion for the (Williams) dealership," Paxton said. There was a barbecue and a band played. Finally, the steam engine was fired up and readied for its last job.

The elder Paxton tied down the steam whistle, and let 'er go. The tractor drove over the edge and its boiler exploded in midair. The tractor bounced off the

canyon wall, then sank silently into the river.
"What would the environmentalists say if that were done today?" Paxton mused.

The Mummy of John Wilkes Booth

History is full of myths and conspiracy theories — and one of these myths pulled into town on the rails and never left.
Shakespearean actor and Confederate secret agent John Wilkes Booth shot President Abraham Lincoln in 1865 at Ford's Theatre in Washington, D.C. Most historians — but not all — agree that Booth was tracked down and killed in a barn in Virginia nearly two weeks later. Booth's body was buried in Green Mount Cemetery in Baltimore, MD.
Others say that government agents killed the wrong man in Garrett's barn. Rumors of his escape from the barn began to circulate even before Booth's body was cold. Some say the body was hastily buried to cover up the government's mistake.
Nearly 40 years later, a man claiming to be John Wilkes Booth committed suicide in Enid, Okla.
"This isn't the story you'll find in textbooks," said Valerie Bowen, director of the Cassia County Historical Museum in Burley.
The man claiming to be Booth turned out to be a drifter who called himself David E. George. George bore a striking resemblance to Booth, and could spout Shakespeare at the drop of a hat.
Some folks in Enid took George's confession seriously. An undertaker embalmed the body, fully expecting that someone from the government or Booth's family would claim it.
But the body — which eventually became mummified — remained unclaimed until an old friend came for it.
The friend, Finis L. Bates, had heard George's story before. Twenty years after Lincoln's assassination, George (who then went by the name John St. Helen) was ill and thought that he would soon be dead. George confessed to Bates, who was a lawyer.
After George recovered, Bates notified the government of St. Helen's confession, but no one seemed interested.
After hearing of George's suicide and mummification, Bates asked a judge in Oklahoma for the body. The judge agreed, thinking that Bates would give his friend a decent burial.
Instead, Bates wrote a book called "The Escape and Suicide of John Wilkes

Booth — Written for the Correction of History" and put the mummy on tour. They say that the mummy made more money on tour than John Wilkes Booth ever did as an actor.

Eventually, the mummy — affectionately known as "John" — was leased to William Evans, the "Carnival King of the Southwest." Evans paid a $40,000 bond, plus a fee of more than $2,000 a year, to display John in what he called the greatest freak-animal show in the country.

After a train wreck destroyed his carnival business, Evans traveled from town to town in a luxury Pullman rail car, charging folks a fee to see the mummified body of "John Wilkes Booth" in a coffin.

Evans later retired, and moved John and the Pullman car to a small potato farm in Declo. He eventually left town with the mummy, but Evans left the Pullman car where it sat.

Evans' Pullman car "has come a long way," said Bowen. Since it was sold, the rail car has been used as a barber shop, a residence and a pig pen.

The rail car was moved from Declo to the Cassia County Historical Museum in Burley a few decades ago, where it was cleaned up and remains on display.

"It's not the plush private car it used to be," said Bowen, "but it's not a pig pen anymore."

The mummy was last seen publicly in 1976, before it was sold to a private collector.

Early Immigrant Jimmy Yamamoto

Jimmy Yamamoto lied to his boss that night in 1915 when he said he was tired and needed to rest.

Yamamoto, 18, had spent three years laboring on a Japanese ship while looking for a chance to slip undetected into the United States.

Under immigration laws at the time, he could not legally enter the U.S.

"I knew if I got caught, that was the end," he told the *Times-News* 66 years later. "Immigration officials stood on the dock, making sure no Orientals left the ships."

When his ship docked at Tacoma, Wash., that night, he saw his chance to escape a life of poverty and start anew in America.

Instead of going to his quarters to rest, Yamamoto, with no money and knowing little English, slid into the water and swam to a pier. Then, under the cover of darkness, he disappeared into the woods.

Yamamoto had planned his daring escape well; he carried in his pockets several valuable silk handkerchiefs he could easily sell for American money.

People "were pretty good to me," he said, giving him food and asking no questions even though they suspected he was from a ship.

He made his way to Seattle, where he took the first job offered to him — in a salmon cannery.

Yamamoto worked numerous jobs over the next two years as he searched for a place to call home. He finally found that place on the Camas Prairie at Fairfield. Harry Geisler hired him to farm there in 1917.

MYCHEL MATTHEWS, TIMES-NEWS PHOTO ILLUSTRATION
Jimmy Yamamoto, seen at age 83 in an illustration made from a 1981 photo, risked everything to enter the United States in 1915.

Meanwhile, Matsuyo Kanno was born in Idaho Falls. Her Issei parents, Yuki and Heiji Kanno, left Japan for Hawaii in the 1890s after their marriage. Yamamoto and Matsuyo, who took the name "Mary," were married in 1931. Yamamoto purchased property in 1941 and began farming for himself. In December that year, the Japanese bombed Pearl Harbor. One of eight Kanno sisters, who lived on the West Coast, had to sell her fine furniture and move to an inland Japanese internment camp.

The Yamamotos were spared that fate.

Eventually, Congress passed legislation allowing people of Japanese birth to become U.S. citizens and Yamamoto became a citizen in 1953. He retired from farming in 1966 and the couple moved to Gooding. Yamamoto died in 1991. Yamamoto was called "James" only in his obituary. His Japanese name is not known.

DeWitt Young, Early Fireman and County Commissioner

The Burrington Hotel at Main Avenue and Third Street East, now known as Idaho Street East, burned down in 1906.

DeWitt Young, a 21-year-old volunteer with the Twin Falls Volunteer Fire Department, responded to the fire alarm that evening.

By the time firemen arrived, "there was no chance of saving the hotel building," Young wrote in the folk-history book of Twin Falls County, compiled for the

HIDDEN HISTORY

Idaho Territorial Centennial in 1963.

Efforts then focused on keeping the Bonham and Peters variety store from going up in flames. The building, with a flat roof and a fire wall, stood a few lots away from the burning hotel.

Men from the fire department, started just months before by Young, Fred Harder Sr. and Jimmy Gallagher, hung blankets over the wall and down the side of the building.

A bucket brigade was started up to the roof to keep the blankets wet.

"I was on the roof pouring water over the blankets as fast as the buckets reached the top, when all of a sudden, a draft from the fire caught the building and shook it violently, just like an earthquake..." Young said. "I staggered to grab the next bucket, thinking every minute that the whole building would topple over right into the raging fire.

"I thought that I was a goner, for sure," he said. The building weaved back and forth, "but she didn't topple. I was scared pink, but glad to be alive."

Forty years later, Young served as a county commissioner.

"One term was enough," he said.

MYCHEL MATTHEWS, TIMES-NEWS PHOTO ILLUSTRATION
Times-News writer Lorayne O. Smith interviewed DeWitt Young, 94, for her weekly feature, "The Elders," in 1979. Patrick Sullivan photographed Young's image in a mirror in his home during the interview.

Marsh Basin, Early Seat of Cassia County

Although early emigrant trails, stage lines and freight routes first bypassed Marsh Basin, the valley quickly became the hub of south-central Idaho.

The Oregon Trail passed north of the basin, nestled in the shadows of Mount Harrison, while the California Trail passed south of Cache Peak and through the City of Rocks.

The Overland Stage and Kelton Freight Line ran north into Idaho from Utah, but both turned west at the City of Rocks, before reaching the basin.

It wasn't long before cattlemen found the basin, with its flowing creeks and abundant meadows.

By 1868, thousands of head of cattle grazed in the region, which then composed eastern Owyhee County.

In 1870, the Kelton Freight Line bypassed the City of Rocks and continued north through Marsh Basin before converging with the Oregon Trail. The following year, homesteader William Vaughn built the first home in the basin. The first "store" in the basin was created the same year, when merchant Andrew Burstrom's wagon became bogged down in the mud. He sold his goods off the wagon and decided to stay. Burstom later built a log store nearby. By 1875, 14 families made the basin their home. Three years later, the City of Rocks home station was abandoned and the stage line was rerouted through Marsh Creek.

In 1876, Rock Creek merchant James Bascom sold his store to Herman Stricker and moved to the basin. Bascom and Miles Robison eventually purchased Burstrom's store and 10 acres of Vaughn's homestead to create a town site.

By the late 1870s, nearly 95 families had settled in the area, 250 miles from the Owyhee County seat at Silver City.

Marsh Basin cattleman and Territorial Rep. Rice Wood, in 1879, introduced a bill to divide the county. Marsh Basin was then proposed as the seat of the new Cassia County, which extended to the present Owyhee County line, a few miles west of Balanced Rock.

The town's name was then changed to the more sophisticated "Albion."

PHOTO COURTESY OF ALBION HISTORICAL SOCIETY
Customers are seen gathered around James Snodgrass, second from the left, at the Snodgrass General Store in 1907.

The Pony Express (Sort of) Came through Here

In 1860, the land that would become Idaho was mostly unoccupied by permanent settlers.

HIDDEN HISTORY

This was still Washington Territory. Gold was yet to be discovered here and civil war was brewing elsewhere.

The threat of war spurred the need for faster communication between the U.S. and the Western frontier. Thus the Pony Express was born.

On April 3, 1860, two Pony Express riders left simultaneously from St. Joseph, MO and Sacramento, CA. Riders made the westbound trip in nine days and 23 hours and the eastbound trip in 11 days and 12 hours.

The short-lived Pony Express consisted of relays of men riding horses carrying saddlebags of mail across a 2000-mile trail.

The mailbags — called *mochilas* (Spanish for knapsack) — were large leather bags with pockets for mail. Riders would throw the *mochila* over the saddle, then sit on it to keep it in place.

The Pony Express had more than 100 stations, 80 riders, and between 400 and 500 horses.

None of these were in Idaho.

"The Pony Express route didn't go anywhere near Idaho, but we know there were 'feeder routes'" that spread north and south from the main route, said Dick DeSchoen, president of the Pony Express National Museum in St. Joseph, MO.

These feeder routes allowed riders with mail from distant places to reach the regular Pony Express riders, DeSchoen said.

In the 1950s, DeSchoen's family bought the land where the original Pony Express office sat in St. Joseph and worked to preserve the property.

The original Pony Express building — which houses the museum — is on the National Register of Historic Places. The museum receives some 40,000 visitors each year, DeSchoen said.

"Many people think they are descendants of Pony Express riders, but my feeling is that many of these were actually riders on the feeder routes," he said.

In Idaho, the feeder routes followed the tried-and-true pioneer trails that had seen travel for 30 years.

The Pony Express service, founded by William H. Russell, William B. Waddell and Alexander Majors, lasted only until Oct. 24, 1861. The completion of the Pacific Telegraph line ended the need for its existence.

Shoshone Ice Cave

Geologists call Shoshone Ice Cave one of Earth's natural wonders.
It's the largest known lava ice cave in the world, extending 1,000 feet deep.
The largest cavern in the ancient lava tube is three blocks long, 30 feet wide

MYCHEL MATTHEWS

PUBLIC DOMAIN
The entrance to Shoshone Ice Caves is seen in this early photograph. The photographer is not identified, but the writing on the photo resembles that of early photographer Charles Savage, who extensively photographed the area in the late 1800s.

and 40 feet high. Tunnels are 90 feet below the surface, keeping the air temperature at a constant 18 to 33 degrees.
Ice forms in the cave as air currents flow through the tubes, causing subterranean water to freeze. It has been said that Shoshoni tribes passing through the area stayed clear, attributing the ice formation at the mouth of the cave to evil spirits.
The cave was discovered in 1880. Early residents of Shoshone harvested ice from the cave, giving the town a reputation as being the only place for hundreds of miles where one could buy a cold beer.
In the mid-1930s, the Works Progress Administration attempted to develop the cave by opening a second entrance. Ice melted rapidly and the project was abandoned.
Geologist Russell Robinson in 1954 reestablished ice formation in the cave.
The cave is on private land 16 miles north of Shoshone on U.S. 75.

Monsters of the River

Before the Magic Valley was settled, Snake River white sturgeon grew to enormous sizes.
Back then, Native American tribes had a special spiritual relationship with the prehistoric fish, said Doug Megargle, regional fisheries manager with the Idaho Department of Fish and Game.
The fish are known to live for 100 years under the right conditions: a pristine river free of dams.
Alex Ghent caught a 1,500-pound sturgeon in 1911 in the river south of Hagerman, using an eel for bait on a seven-inch hook and a cord line, Lloyd E.

HIDDEN HISTORY

PHOTO COURESTY CLARENCE E. BISBEE, TWIN FALLS COUNTY HISTORICAL MUSEUM
A Snake River white sturgeon is seen draped over a car in this early Clarence E. Bisbee photo. These prehistoric monsters may live up to 100 years.

Byrne wrote in his book "Buhl as It Was."
Ghent weighed the giant freshwater fish on the Byrne family's hay scale.
Since the development of irrigation and reservoirs on the Snake River, the sturgeons' population — and size — has dwindled. The ancient bottom-feeder needs a free-flowing river to spawn, Megargle said.
Today, anglers still catch sturgeon in the Snake River, but with barbless hooks and on a catch-and-release basis.

Frank Gooding: Why Magic Valley is in Mountain Time Zone

Frank R. Gooding was an English immigrant, who, in 1888, settled in the area that would eventually bear his name.
Gooding was elected to the Idaho Legislature 10 years later and was elected governor of Idaho in 1904, all before he became a U.S. citizen. During his two terms as governor, the Idaho Capitol was built in Boise.
As governor, Gooding proclaimed Thursday, Nov. 28, 1907, as Thanksgiving, and encouraged Idahoans to "refrain from their usual vocation, and in their homes and places of worship offer acknowledgement to God for His

many blessings, and prayers for the continuance of His divine favor."
Gooding, a Republican, was known to have an abrasive personality and often clashed with other members of his party.
He was elected Idaho's U.S. Senator in 1920. At that time, most of the state — including the Magic Valley — was in the Pacific Time Zone. Gooding sponsored a bill in the Senate to place all of Idaho south of the Salmon River in the Mountain Time Zone.
He died in office in 1928 and is buried in Elmwood Cemetery in Gooding. Some from the Magic Valley have claimed Gooding would have run for the presidency had he lived.

PUBLIC DOMAIN
Frank Robert Gooding was the governor of Idaho from January 1905 to January 1909. Twenty years later, Gooding served as Idaho's U.S. Senator.

The Mormon Trail

Seven paths led west in the 19th century: the Lewis and Clark Trail, the Santa Fe Trail, the Oregon-California Trail, the Mormon Trail, the Pony Express, the Transcontinental Telegraph and the Transcontinental Railroad.
Of the emigrant trails, the Mormon Trail was the longest.
After Joseph Smith, the founder of the Church of Jesus Christ of Latter-day Saints, was imprisoned in 1844 in Carthage, Ill., and was killed when a mob stormed the jailhouse, remaining church officials searched for a refuge in the western frontier, far away from criticism and persecution.
The church by then had gathered a large following in the United States, but an even larger group of coverts waited overseas.
"The Mormon Trail of those years stretched all the way from Liverpool to Salt Lake City, making it by far the longest of any trail west," wrote Arthur King Peters in his book "Seven Trails West."
In the 30 years between 1847 and 1877, 85,000 Mormons settled in the Salt Lake area. About 70,000 of those were Europeans, mainly from England and Wales.

HIDDEN HISTORY

COURTESY PHOTO
Harrison Reynolds Matthews, center, known as Bish, brought his young bride to Oakley from Grantsville, Utah, in the early 1880s. Bish was the great-grandfather of Times-News *reporter Mychel Matthews. Her grandfather, Thomas Earl Matthews, stands to the left of his father in this photograph, taken around 1900 in Oakley.*

COURTESY PHOTO
William Matthews, great-great-grandfather of Times-News *reporter Mychel Matthews, was born in 1818 in England. He and his first wife were converted to Mormonism about 1850.*

The Mormon emigrant ship Amazon left the London dock in 1863 with Charles Dickens aboard to record the trip.

"I... had come aboard this emigrant ship to see what eight hundred Latter-day Saints were like," Dickens wrote.

In 1847, Brigham Young declared the Salt Lake Valley as the new home to Mormons. In 1849, the Provisional State of Deseret — a large region around Utah extending north from Los Angeles and San Diego into Oregon, east into Wyoming and Colorado, and south into New Mexico and Arizona — was formed by the church.

Starting in 1850, Congress started whittling away at the proposed state and changed the territory's name to Utah. But that didn't stop the church from "colonizing" towns outside the area.

Oakley was one of these towns, settled by Mormons from the Grantsville, Utah, area in the early 1880s.

Twin Falls County's 1st Elected Sheriff

On March 18, 1907, Twin Falls County got its first sheriff, appointed by county commissioners.

George Aiken served for two years and opted out at election time in 1908. His replacement was chosen at the county's first general election in November

PHOTO COURTESY OF CLARENCE E. BISBEE, TWIN FALLS COUNTY HISTORICAL MUSEUM
The mining town of Jarbidge, Nev., is seen in this early C.E. Bisbee photo.

that year.
The county didn't have to look far for a qualified candidate. Deputy Charles Dyer was the town marshal before Aikens recruited him for the sheriff's office. He served as both the marshal and deputy until the town could hire his replacement.
Dyer became sheriff in January 1909 and he took his job seriously.
"When a stranger came to town, Sheriff Dyer was quick to question him," reads "Lawmen, the History of Idaho Sheriffs 1863-2000," a book compiled by the Idaho Sheriffs' Association. "If (a stranger) didn't have proper identification and no purpose in town, he was booked into the county jail on a suspicious character charge. After six to 10 days of detention, he was released and encouraged to 'fit' or 'git.'"
When transporting prisoners to the county jail — a cave in Rock Creek Canyon — became a nuisance, Dyer made arrangements to rent the town's jail until the new courthouse and jail on Shoshone Street was finished in 1911.
Dyer "was one of the ablest officers that the county ever had," Aikens told the *Twin Falls Times* after Dyer's death. "He was a natural detective and possessed unusual ability in detecting criminals."
Dyer served one term as sheriff before running for county assessor. He later became despondent and became a miner. He shot himself in February 1917, while sitting in his tent in Jarbidge, Nev.

Remnants of Peavey's Whistle Stop

Two miles west of Filer, a whistle post stands along U.S. 30, a reminder of a community long gone.
Peavey was a whistle stop on the railroad, said Filer historian Peggy Cristobal. Many westbound travelers found themselves walking back to Filer from Peavey after falling asleep on the train and missing their stop.
Peavey was named for a pioneer family whose home housed the post office

HIDDEN HISTORY

for their neighbors. Elizabeth Peavey was the postmistress.

Her husband was prominent businessman Arthur J. Peavey, who started Twin Falls Title and Abstract Co. in 1907.

When the couple moved to Twin Falls, Elizabeth turned the post office over to their son who ran a store in Peavey.

COURTESY PHOTO
Elizabeth Peavey, postmistress of Peavey, poses by the whistle post near her home two miles west of Filer.

Execution or Lynching?

Idaho in 1863 included the area that would later become Montana and most of Wyoming. The population base — mostly gold miners chasing dreams of wealth — was in the Clearwater region in what is now the Idaho panhandle. Lloyd MacGruder was murdered on Oct. 11, 1863, along what later became known as the "MacGruder Corridor" near the Selway River in northern Idaho. Less than five months later, James Romaine, Daniel Howard and Christopher Lowery were hanged at Lewiston — the territorial capital — for the brutal murder of the widely known pack-train operator and four of his men.
Arthur Hart, past director of the Idaho State Historical Society, called the hangings "the first legal executions" in Idaho's history.
Others disagree. MacGruder and his men were murdered before Idaho had any laws, they say.
Territories had little control over their own affairs, wrote former University of Idaho professor Carlos A. Schwantes in his book "In Mountain Shadows." Territories were controlled by the federal government and officiated by appointees of the president. William H. Wallace, an old friend of President Abraham Lincoln, was appointed Idaho's first territorial governor in March 1863.
MacGruder and his men were murdered seven months later, several months before the first session of territorial lawmakers convened.
So were the hangings legal executions — or lynchings?

Stagecoaches in the Magic Valley

Magic Valley mass transit in the late 19th century meant riding "Stagecoach King" Ben Holladay's coaches from the train depot in Kelton, Utah, into Idaho Territory.
Holladay's stage line ran through the City of Rocks and Oakley before arriving at the Rock Creek Station south of present-day Hansen.
Once folks started to make their homes in the area, other stage lines offered service between the new towns.
C.C. "Uncle Charlie" Haynes, a pioneer who spent more than 50 years in the stagecoach business, carried mail from mines in the Wood River Valley over Galena Summit to Sawtooth City.
Later, Haynes started his own stage line north of the Snake River, carrying people from the depot at Shoshone to Shoshone Falls.
Twin Falls founder I.B. Perrine ran his stage business, Twin Falls-Jerome Stage Line, from an office in the Hotel Perrine at the west corner of Main Avenue and Shoshone Street. Perrine's stages also carried tourists to Shoshone Falls.

PHOTO COURTESY OF CLARENCE E. BISBEE, TWIN FALLS COUNTY HISTORICAL MUSEUM
The Twin Falls-Jerome Stagecoach is seen in front of the Hotel Perrine in downtown Twin Falls in this early Clarence E. Bisbee photograph.

I.B. Perrine's 'Town House'

In 1883, I.B. Perrine settled in the Snake River Canyon near the Blue Lakes. He farmed hundreds of acres on both sides of the canyon.
A few years after founding Twin Falls in 1904, Perrine built his "town house" at Shoshone Street and Sixth Avenue North, kitty-corner from City Park.
The home faced the old Twin Falls High School, which later became O'Leary Junior High.
Perrine's friend Bob McCollum lived behind him, at Shoshone Street and Seventh Avenue North. Their backyards joined at the alley.
Perrine's house was replaced by the First Christian Church. Rumor has it, the house was moved to Filer.

PHOTO COURTESY OF F.W. SHEELOR, TWIN FALLS COUNTY HISTORICAL MUSEUM
I.B. Perrine's 'town house' is seen in 1912 on Sixth Avenue and Shoshone Street North, kitty-corner from City Park. The First Christian Church sits on that corner today. Photographer F.W. Sheelor built the panoramic camera used to produce this image.

Hollister, a 'New' Municipality

Some towns take a while to organize.
The first land drawing for lots near Hollister took place in 1908 in Twin Falls, before the Salmon Dam was completed. The second land drawing was held more than a year later on Main Street in Hollister.
The town incorporated on March 9, 1917. But its Certificate of Municipal Incorporation was signed by Idaho Secretary of State Pete Cenarrusa on July 29, 1998.
The town was named for Chicago investment broker Harry Hollister, who heavily invested in the Salmon Tract in the early 20th century.

PHOTO COURTESY OF CLARENCE E. BISBEE, TWIN FALLS COUNTY HISTORICAL MUSEUM
Men register for the 1909 land drawing on Main Street in Hollister.

PHOTO COURTESY OF CLARENCE E. BISBEE, TWIN FALLS COUNTY HISTORICAL MUSEUM
Men register for the Hollister land drawing on Main Street.

The Minidoka Relocation Center

Driven by wartime hysteria after Japan bombed Pearl Harbor, the U.S. government rounded up some 13,000 people of Japanese descent and "relocated" them from their homes on the West Coast to a desolate internment camp in south-central Idaho.
The camp, located in Jerome County about 7 miles north of Eden, was known as the "Minidoka Internment Camp" or the "Minidoka Relocation Center." But to locals, it was the "Hunt Camp."
The camp, which operated from August 1942 to October 1945, encompassed nearly 1,000 acres and included 600 buildings, 5 miles of barbed wire fencing and eight guard towers.
The various names of the camp are confusing to most.
Some say the name of the camp came from Minidoka County, which borders Jerome County. There also is a tiny town called Minidoka in eastern Minidoka County, far from the internment camp.
Some maps — even the "you-are-here" maps at the Minidoka camp ruins — point to the town of Minidoka as the internment site.
Actually, Minidoka predates both the county and the town. It's an Indian word the government used to refer to a 1903 federal irrigation project north of the Snake River near the present-day town of Rupert.
The Minidoka Relocation Center is within the U.S. Bureau of Reclamation's Minidoka Project.
Some say the camp's unofficial name, Hunt, was named for a now-defunct town located near there before World War II. Others say the Hunt Camp

HIDDEN HISTORY

COURTESY PHOTO
Minidoka Relocation Center near Eden was constructed in the summer of 1942.

COURTESY PHOTO
Black lava stone marks the site of a guardhouse at the Minidoka National Historic Site near Eden, where thousands of Japanese Americans were detained in the internment camp during World War II.

was named for Frank W. Hunt, the governor of Idaho from 1901 to 1903, who established Idaho State University in Pocatello. Neither of those ideas seem plausible. According to an archaeological survey of the site completed in 2001, "no features or artifacts predating the relocation center were encountered" during the inspection of the monument — with the exception of the North Side irrigation canal built in 1906. The Hunt name was more likely a shout-out to Wilson Price Hunt and his party of explorers who traveled through southern Idaho in 1811, says Linda Helms, with the Jerome County Historical Society.

No town called Hunt ever existed in the area, Helms said, but some of the Hunt party did camp near the site on their way to Astoria in Oregon Country. According to U.S. Department of Interior documents, Hunt was the post office designation used at that time for homes in that area.

A few acres of ruins are left at the site, now listed on the National Register of Historic Places.

At the end of the WWII, the camp was dismantled and buildings were moved from the site. The land was given to soldiers needing farmland after they returned from the war.

The Twin Falls American Legion Hall

In 1919, the Magic Valley welcomed home hundreds who fought in World War I.

In April that year, 10,000 residents filled Shoshone Street, from City Park to the Twin Falls Depot, to greet 250 soldiers as they arrived by train, according to the *Twin Falls Daily News*.

Also that year, the American Legion was chartered as "a patriotic veterans organization devoted to mutual helpfulness," and a local post was endorsed. The legion, which evolved from a group of war-weary veterans of the Great War into one of the most influential nonprofit groups in the U.S., was especially active during the 1920s.

Twin Falls built its American Legion Hall in 1926 in the 300 block of Hansen Street East, about a block and a half from City Park. The building is now owned by the city of Twin Falls and is used to house the city engineering department, and planning and zoning.

PHOTO COURTESY OF CLARENCE E. BISBEE, TWIN FALLS COUNTY HISTORICAL MUSEUM

The American Legion Hall was built in 1926 on Hansen Street East in Twin Falls. The entrance of the building faced the alley that runs between Third Avenue East and Fourth Avenue, as it does today.

Opera in Twin Falls

Movie houses "are fast becoming almost as numerous as cigar stores or confectionery stands," the *Twin Falls News* reported in 1907.

HIDDEN HISTORY

PHOTO COURTESY OF TWIN FALLS COUNTY HISTORICAL MUSEUM
In February 1912, local talent performed the Japanese opera 'The Mikado' in the Lyric Theater -- the first opera performed in Twin Falls.

And by 1910, founding fathers thought the new village was ready for live opera.

I.B. Perrine invited a Mr. Grant, who managed the Salt Lake Theatrical Circuit, to check out the possibility of building a grand opera house in Twin Falls. After assessing the situation, Grant told a group gathered in Perrine's office that he believed the town "could support such an enterprise," reported the Feb. 3, 1910, edition of the *Twin Falls Weekly News*.

A three-story opera house was to be built behind the Hotel Perrine, at Shoshone Street and Second Avenue West, for $150,000. The men planned to have the "splendid," "fully modern" building finished by the following September.

The opera house never materialized, and the newspaper never mentioned it again.

Two years later, local talent performed "The Mikado", a Japanese opera in two acts, at the Lyric Theater in Twin Falls.

MYCHEL MATTHEWS

The Bucket of Blood Saloon

Early residents fought hard on both sides of prohibition, long before the 18th Amendment.

City trustees canvassed the new village of Twin Falls, deciding residents wanted few saloons in town.

The Bucket of Blood saloon, one of the first establishments in town, was operated by George Bassett. The Bucket of Blood -- also known as the Headquarters Saloon -- developed an early reputation.

"The saloon had four methods of parting an individual from his money," wrote City Trustee S.T. Hamilton. "First, by the sale of liquid refreshments; second, by permitting him to sit in a poker game; third, by feeding him in the dining room; and fourth, by 'rolling' him in the corral at the alley extension."

On April 28, 1905, Twin Falls city trustees met for the first time after the village incorporated. The first order of business was to set an exorbitant fee for liquor licenses, in hopes of discouraging saloon business.

Trustees fixed the annual price of a liquor license at $2,000 — equal to about $50,000 today — predicting it would drive saloons outside the city limits.

In addition, city trustees approved ordinances restricting saloon business:

- Saloons must close between 10 p.m. and 7 a.m. weekdays and all day Sunday.
- No blinds or screens were permitted.
- No wine rooms were prohibited.
- Women were not allow to enter saloons between 7 p.m. and 7 a.m.

Two days after the city meeting, Dan Kingsley, who operated the ferry at Shoshone Falls, got drunk and drowned in the Snake River, further fueling the prohibition debate.

Meanwhile, barkeepers held their ground, refusing to pay the new liquor license fee.

Bassett, R.W. Jones, Jack Cunningham, S.G. Hamburg, W.S. McQueen and R.W. Carter were charged with selling liquor without a license. Carter was tried first and was found guilty.

At the May meeting, trustees offered the other barkeepers resolution: pay $500 for the next three months while the validity of the liquor ordinance is tested. The five men paid the fee under protest.

Afterward, the men agreed to pay $500 quarterly instead of a $2,000 lump sum, which satisfied the court, according to the *Twin Falls Weekly News*.

Later, police officers raided the basement of the Bucket of Blood and confiscated all gambling devices, including gaming tables, cards and

HIDDEN HISTORY

PHOTO COURTESY OF CLARENCE E. BISBEE, TWIN FALLS COUNTY HISTORICAL MUSEUM

The back of the Hotel Perrine, at the west corner of Shoshone Street and Main Avenue West, is seen in this early Clarence E. Bisbee photograph. Obscured from view by the hotel is the Bucket of Blood Saloon, at the east corner of Shoshone Street and Second Avenue East. The saloon was in rear the building, which fronted Second Avenue.

furnishings. They piled the items and several loads of sagebrush several blocks away. The pile went up in flames the next morning, according to Hamilton. The Bucket of Blood saloon burned down sometime between May and October 1905, according to DeWitt Young, whose family owned the Young and Sons general store at the front of the saloon. Young came to town Oct. 12, 1905, and the Bucket of Blood had gone up in smoke before he arrived. Along with the saloon, Bassett had a restaurant and livery stable at the location.

Most reports put the saloon near the east corner of Shoshone Street and Second Avenue East.

In 1906, a local chapter of the decades-old Women's Christian Temperance Union was organized to create a "sober and pure world," according to its publications, and momentum for prohibition increased.

The Twin Falls County Taxpayers' League unsuccessfully tried to stop the movement, citing the loss of needed revenues from liquor licenses.

In November 1909, Twin Falls County voted to abolish liquor and saloons in the county closed by February 1910. In 1916, the entire state of Idaho went "dry." The 18th Amendment to the U.S. Constitution was ratified in January 1919 and took effect the following year.

Photographer Charles R. Savage

Clarence Bisbee wasn't the only photographer to capture pioneer life in the Magic Valley.
Charles Roscoe Savage was a Mormon who emigrated from England in 1855. He is well known for his photographs of the American West.
Savage settled in Salt Lake City in 1960, then traveled extensively while under contract with the Union Pacific Railroad. He photographed completion of

PHOTO COURTESY OF C.R. SAVAGE, BRIGHAM YOUNG UNIVERSITY LIBRARY
A ferry and the Oregon Short Line Bridge over the Snake River between Burley and Heyburn are seen in this early C.R. Savage photograph.

the transcontinental railroad at Promontory Point on May 10, 1869, where the Union and Central Pacific railroads famously joined in Utah Territory.
Many of his photographs were reproduced in *Harper's Weekly*. Unfortunately, most of his early originals were lost in an 1883 fire at his studio.
Savage had photographed much of the landscape around southern Idaho before Bisbee arrived in 1906.

PHOTO COURTESY OF C.R. SAVAGE, BRIGHAM YOUNG UNIVERSITY LIBRARY
Alpheus Creek is in the foreground of this Charles R. Savage photograph. Bryan Point rises above I.B. Perrine's Blue Lakes Ranch.

Death Valley Scotty

Walter E. "Scotty" Scott, later known as "Death Valley Scotty," left his home in Kentucky at the age of 11. In 1883, Scotty joined his brothers Lynn and George

HIDDEN HISTORY

PHOTO COURTESY OF TWIN FALLS COUNTY HISTORICAL MUSEUM
Walter Scott, later known as "Death Valley Scotty" lived in southern Idaho as a teenager in the 1880s.

in Idaho.

George was a cook for cattle crews and lived at the mouth of Rock Creek Canyon at the base of the South Hills. Lynn was a horseman and made his home in Hagerman.

At age 16, Scotty joined Buffalo Bill Cody's Wild West Show as a stunt rider. He toured the U.S. and Europe with the show from 1888 to 1900, when he married Ella Josephine Milius in New York City. Scotty and Jack, as he called his wife, moved to Cripple Creek, Colo., where he tried unsuccessfully to start a gold mine.

Scotty soon conned a wealthy New York businessman into backing a fictitious gold mine operation. The businessman invested more than $5,000 — equal to $120,000 today — in the mine, but never received any ore.

Eventually, Scotty traveled to New York with a bag supposedly containing $12,000 in gold dust. When he reached his destination, Scotty claimed the bag had been stolen. Newspapers picked up the story and Scotty began a spree of

self-promotion ventures.
In 1905, Scotty made a name for himself by breaking the cross-country speed record in a train known as the "Scott Special" consisting of an engine, baggage car, sleeper and dining car. He left Los Angeles on July 9, and arrived in Chicago less than 45 hours later, breaking an earlier record of 53 hours. Once again, photos of Scotty were splashed across the front pages of national newspapers.
Over the years, Scotty continued to con more investors in gold mine schemes and used many ruses to evade investigators. In 1906, Scotty played himself in a Seattle theater production about his life. He was arrested on various charges of fraud after the play finished, but was eventually released on a technicality.
Scotty upped the ante in his game and leased a mine in the Humbolt Mountains as a front to fence high-grade ore he stole from other mines.
In 1912, he announced that he had sold his mine for $12 million. His creditors sued Scotty after he made this claim and he ended up in jail.
Scotty managed to remain friends with investor Albert Johnson, who had dropped thousands of dollars into his schemes. Johnson purchased several ranches in Death Valley, setting up Scotty for life.
Johnson built a castle in Death Valley, Calif. for a vacation home, but Scotty claimed it was his. It is known as "Scotty's Castle."
Scotty died in 1954 and is buried on the grounds of Scotty's Castle in Death Valley National Park.

The Shoshone Falls Bridge

The original Hansen Bridge, built in 1919, was the first rim-to-rim span across the Snake River Canyon.
It preceded the I.B. Perrine Memorial Bridge, first known as the Jerome-Twin Falls Intercounty Bridge, by nearly a decade.
While engineer R.M. Murray was building the Hansen Bridge, he came up with another idea: to span the canyon just below Shoshone Falls.
On May 1, 1919, Twin Falls County commissioners, led by Chairman T.E. Moore, and Murray inspected the site about one-third of a mile below the falls and declared the plan "feasible," according to the next day's edition of the *Twin Falls Daily News*.
"The Snake River Canyon will be spanned at Shoshone Falls with one of the largest suspension bridges in the United States, forming at once a connecting link of large commercial possibilities between the north and south side counties and affording a new and unique view of the waterfall of immense

scenic possibilities ..." the article says.

At 1,143 feet long, the bridge would have been nearly twice the length of the Hansen Bridge and would have cost $350,000 — about $5 million in today's money.

Murray proposed charging tolls, which he said would pay for the bridge in 15 years.

Eight-inch cables hanging from 120-foot-tall towers at both rims would have suspended the bridge about 400 feet above the river.

The bridge never was built. Neither was the railroad bridge similarly proposed for the same location.

PHOTO COURTESY OF CLARENCE E. BISBEE, TWIN FALLS COUNTY HISTORICAL MUSEUM
The spray from Shoshone Falls is seen in the distance in this Clarence E. Bisbee photograph. Pillar Falls is in the foreground. In 1919, Twin Falls County commissioners considered building a rim-to-rim bridge over the canyon about one-third of a mile below Shoshone Falls.

The Methodist Church on Shoshone Street

Kitty-corner from the county courthouse sits the Twin Falls First United Methodist Church, an impressive structure made of sandstone.

The church, however, had humble beginnings.

It started as Twin Falls' first schoolhouse on Third Avenue East, a few blocks from its present location on Shoshone Street East.

In 1906, the Methodist Episcopal congregation relocated the 24-by-30 wooden structure to Fourth Avenue East near Shoshone Street, across the street from City Park. The building was moved, papered and painted at a cost of $577.

Two years later, the congregation gave the chapel a facelift. The addition of sharply pointed Gothic arches and a facade made with Boise white sand-lime brick completely changed its appearance.

As the congregation grew, it made plans to expand the building into the empty lot next door, at the south corner of Fourth and Shoshone.

Twin Falls pioneer photographer Clarence E. Bisbee recorded the laying of the cornerstone of the addition in 1916. The congregation remodeled the existing building and added a massive brown sandstone sanctuary, tripling the size of the building and increasing its capacity to 1,150.

Contractor Earl Felt built the sanctuary, designed in the Tudor Gothic style by

PHOTO COURTESY OF CLARENCE E. BISBEE, TWIN FALLS COUNTY HISTORICAL MUSEUM
The cornerstone of the Methodist Episcopal Church, at Shoshone Street and Fourth Avenue East, was laid in 1916.

architect B. Morgan Nesbit. Steeply parapeted gables and stone tracery set with stained glass are its distinct features. One of the windows was a memorial to Bishop Luccock and the other a contribution by the Epworth League, according to the *Twin Falls Weekly News*.

Dedicatory services were held in October 1917 and featured a 12-piece orchestra led by R.A. Parrott. An $18,000 building debt remained when the church opened, but by the end of the service, the congregation had pledged enough to clear the debt. In addition, T.F. Warner and horseman Charlie McMaster donated $2,000 each for a new pipe organ.

The building was said to be worth $60,000.

A stained-glass dome, designed by John Visser, architect of the nearby Presbyterian Church, was built over the church's large auditorium in 1920.

Tom Bell's Long Plunge

Shoshone Falls, on the Snake River, has long been compared with Niagara Falls. But not until a small boat full of miners went over the falls in 1881 did the spot became a bona fide tourist attraction.

Gold was discovered in the Snake River Canyon in 1869. A mining camp called Shoshone City soon cropped up in the canyon above Shoshone Falls.

Charles Walgamott opened a tent hotel and restaurant on the north side of the river above the falls in 1876. A couple of years later, Irishman Thomas Bell built a cabin directly across the river.

In his book "Six Decades Back," Walgamott called Bell a loner who sat in the doorway of his cabin and played his fiddle — when he wasn't searching for gold.

Bell was a bit of a "Johnny-come-lately," for he came to Shoshone Falls during the end of the gold rush to the Snake River, said Philip Homan, an associate professor at Idaho State University.

Bell would launch his little boat into the river at his cabin and cross the current to an island above Bridal Veil Falls, near the brink of Shoshone Falls. He would spend his days on his island gathering gold with a pick, shovel and rocker before venturing home each evening.

Upstream from Bell Island, as it later became known, 500 Chinese miners worked the river at Shoshone City.

In June 1881, Homan reports, several Chinese miners ran into Bell at Stricker Store, a trading post on the Old Oregon Trail south of present-day Hansen. The men asked Bell, known for his boating skills, to ferry them and their goods across the river to their camp on the north bank above the falls.

PHOTO COURTESY OF CLARENCE E. BISBEE, TWIN FALLS COUNTY HISTORICAL MUSEUM

In 1881, Irish miner Tom Bell lost control of his boat in the Snake River immediately above Shoshone Falls and was swept over the falls to his death, also killing the four miners who were his passengers. Bell's body was found, but none of the miners' bodies ever surfaced.

Bell agreed, but his attempt to cross the river in the overloaded boat would be his last. "Whether he had become careless from tempting the waves so often, or whether he lost or broke an oar, will never be known," wrote the *Salt Lake Tribune* in 1883. "But one thing is certain — that he and all the contents of the boat went over the falls, going down 200 feet and sinking to rise no more." Bell's body was retrieved from the river, but the bodies of his passengers never were found.

Walgamott gathered Bell's mining tools and fragments of his boat and placed them in Bell's cabin as a memorial to the 37-year-old miner.

While Idaho's "Niagara of the West" was not unknown to tourists before Bell's untimely demise, "the death of Tom Bell gave Shoshone Falls an atmosphere of morbid fascination that made them Idaho's first tourist attraction," Homan said.

Anna Daly, Buhl's First Elected Woman School Trustee

Anna Daly was the first woman elected to the Buhl School Board. She also was the first trustee to lose the position before taking office.

In the Sept. 5, 1933, school trustee election, two incumbents, H. G. Schaefer and W.R. Hatfield, filed for re-election. Grant Miller and Anna Daly, wife of E.J. Daly, also filed as candidates.

Hatfield was considered a shoo-in. In his 12 years on the board, the school district's indebtedness had been slashed from $384,000 to $110,000. The

HIDDEN HISTORY

PHOTO COURTESY OF CLARENCE E. BISBEE, TWIN FALLS COUNTY HISTORICAL MUSEUM
The Buhl School is seen in this early Clarence E. Bisbee photograph.

district, at the beginning of the 1933-34 school year, had cash reserves of $28,000, according to the *Buhl Herald*.
Schaefer, who had been in office only two years, hoped to be re-elected by claiming to have supported Hatfield's efforts.
Voters cast 210 votes to re-elect Hatfield, but snubbed Schaefer and Miller. Daly received a stunning 190 votes that day, announced the *Buhl Herald*, beating Schaefer, Miller and write-in candidate Mrs. L.G. Lacy for the trustee position.
A week later, the *Herald* declared the school election to be a "fluke."
At the time, Idaho law required a majority vote in school elections. Votes for Daly — 48 percent of the 397 votes cast — came just nine votes shy of a majority. The school board and Maude Kleinkopf, Twin Falls County school superintendent, determined that Daly's election was not valid.
Kleinkopf refused to appoint a replacement, saying she was not confident of the legal stipulations for appointment. Idaho State Attorney General Bert Miller, however, said the decision was Kleinkopf's.
Kleinkopf then surprised voters by naming Harry Wilson, the local jeweler to fill the position. It was another 40 years before another woman was elected to the Buhl School Board. Theda McManaman was elected in May 1973.

A Few Words from the Buhl School Superintendent

In 1919, the town of Buhl was barely a dozen years old, but its school system was well established.
By then, the school district already had three grade schools and a high school. Superintendent J. Henry Allen wrote about his school system in a Dec. 11, 1919, article in the *Buhl Herald*.
The F.H. Buhl School — named for Frank Buhl, a major investor in the Twin Falls South Side Irrigation Tract — was the first substantial schoolhouse built in Buhl.
Buhl, president of Buhl Steel Co. of Sharon, Pa., donated $25,000 toward construction of the building. The district in 1909 bonded $10,000 to complete the project.
The F.H. Buhl School housed all 12 grades. Three years later, Buhl High School was built and later became Lincoln School.
In 1912, the F.H. Buhl School housed only elementary classes.
But by 1919, 32 teachers were employed by the Buhl School District, including a supervisor of art and music and a school nurse who taught physiology and hygiene.
"The practical side of education is duly stressed," wrote Allen, adding that a blend "of the cultural and practical is necessary for truly symmetrical development."
The Buhl education offered girls courses in Domestic Sciences and Domestic Arts.
"A girl who has taken our Domestic Science work will make a far better housekeeper than a girl without this training," Allen said.
The Domestic Arts department was geared toward an appreciation of "what good clothes are, and... how to make... garments properly, to trim a hat artistically, and to dress in good taste.
"The course is something that every girl should know," he said.
Hot lunches were prepared in part by the "girls of the Domestic Science classes as a part of their regular work," Allen said, which kept school meals at a reasonable price.
Teachers taught language, science and math, as well as shorthand, typewriting, penmanship and bookkeeping.
"The teachers do not run off after every new fad in education," Allen said, "but rather believe in trying out standard methods of instruction and generally follow the old adage: 'Be not the first by whom the new are tried; nor yet the last to lay the old aside.'"

HIDDEN HISTORY

Fighting Fires in Twin Falls

There weren't enough buckets in town to put out a house fire in the old days. So in 1906, the Twin Falls Investment Co. donated a building and two lots for a fire station at Shoshone Street and Third Avenue North. Two 15-man hose carts with 500-foot hoses then were purchased for $110 each.

The Twin Falls Volunteer Fire Department, consisting of two companies of 20 men each, officially organized the following spring and moved into the new station.

But in 1908, the fire station burned down.

That year, voters approved a bond to build and equip a fire station for $10,000. The new station was built in front of the jailhouse at 240 Second Ave. S., and a new horse-drawn steam fire engine was purchased for $5,986, more than the station cost to build. Fire Chief J.P. Taggart was hired at $15 per month.

In 1910, a smaller, paid fire department replaced the larger volunteer outfit.

In 1921, the fire department replaced its 1908 steam fire engine with a new American-LaFrance Triple Combination Pump Engine and Hose Motor Car that cost $20,000.

In 1935, the department increased its

PHOTO COURTESY OF CLARENCE E. BISBEE, TWIN FALLS COUNTY HISTORICAL MUSEUM
Twin Falls Volunteer Fire Department bought this horse-drawn steam engine fire wagon in 1910.

PHOTO COURTESY OF CLARENCE E. BISBEE, TWIN FALLS COUNTY HISTORICAL MUSEUM
The Twin Falls Investment Co. donated a building and two lots at Shoshone and Third Avenue North in 1906. The building burned down in 1908.

workforce to eight paid firemen. A decade later, it became first in the state to adopt a "three-platoon system" with firemen working 56 hours a week, instead of 84 hours a week under a two-shift system.

A new station, designed by architect Harald Gerber, was built on Second Avenue East next to City Hall.

Hailey, Seat of 2 Counties

The Idaho Territorial Legislature created Alturas County, an enormous area north of the Snake River, in 1864.

Though the county covered all of modern-day Elmore, Camas, Blaine, Ada and Owyhee counties, much of Clark, Jefferson, Custer, Power, Bingham and Bonneville counties, and some of Boise, Lemhi and Fremont counties, few towns existed in it.

By 1881, county seat Rocky Bar, originally a mining boomtown of 2,500 people, was failing. When the Legislature put the decision to move the county seat into the hands of Alturas County voters, people in the new town of Bellevue in the Wood River Valley thought their town was a shoo-in.

But Indian fighter, rancher, miner, stage company owner, statesman and land speculator John Hailey had a different idea.

Backed by eastern investors, Hailey picked out 440 acres between Ketchum and Bellevue, and laid out a townsite and a campaign to populate it. Hailey advertised the new town as the "Denver of Idaho."

A bitter rivalry developed between the towns of Hailey and Bellevue in the race to become the county seat. It's said the election was fraught with fraud on both sides. Town supporters were encouraged to "vote early and often," according to Sandra Hofferber's book "A Pictorial Early History of the Wood River Valley."

"Charges and counter charges were leveled, court suits were threatened, and, finally help was sent from the Idaho Territorial Governor," Hofferber wrote.

In the end, Hailey was declared the winner.

In 1884, John Hailey was elected a territorial delegate. In 1900, he became the chairman of the Central Committee of the Democratic Party when Idaho became a state.

Meanwhile, the territorial legislature started to whittle away at Alturas County. In 1889, Elmore and Logan counties were cut away from Alturas County. Bellevue became part of Logan County and became its county seat.

Two years later, after Idaho became a state, the legislature attempted to return Bellevue to Alturas County by creating two new counties from Alturas and Logan. The Idaho Supreme Court struck down the measure.

HIDDEN HISTORY

The legislature, in 1895, recombined Alturas and Logan counties, creating Blaine County. Hailey remained the county seat. Two weeks later, it divided Lincoln County — with Shoshone as its county seat — from Blaine County, named for Republican Sen. James G. Blaine, of Maine, who unsuccessfully ran for president in 1884.

PUBLIC DOMAIN
John Hailey, the founder of Hailey, is seen in this undated photo with his wife, Louis, and son, George.

The Riverside Inn at Milner

After the South Side Irrigation Project was completed, attention turned to the project on the north side of the Snake River.
The once-booming town of Milner — population 1,500 — was temporarily revived as men returned to work on the North Side Canal in 1908.
Brothers James S. and W.S. Kuhn of Pittsburgh, developers of the Twin Falls North Side Land and Water Co., purchased land in Milner for a grand hotel.
The Riverside Inn, designed by Wayland and Fennel, of Boise, was a three-story 70-by-80 building with a full basement.
The hotel, which opened in May 1908, boasted all the modern comforts, including plumbing and electricity. Each of the 40 sleeping rooms was heated by steam. Elaborate chandeliers hung in every room. Six of the rooms were fancy suites with private baths.
The hotel was connected to the town water supply and the grounds were landscaped and included tennis courts and a dance pavilion.
A resort for tourists and businessmen, the hotel was the social center of the area. But it stood for only 15 years.
The Kuhn brothers' business went into receivership in 1913. The town and the

hotel fell on hard times as businesses left the Milner area and tourists stopped coming.

PHOTO COURTESY OF CLARENCE E. BISBEE, TWIN FALLS COUNTY HISTORICAL MUSEUM
The Riverside Inn, with its tennis courts and dance pavilion, opened in 1908 during the construction of the North Side Canal.

James H. Grenzebeck, of Jerome, was contracted to raze the building in 1923. The lumber and materials were salvaged and used to build the Murtaugh Hotel, a few miles downstream from Milner. It is not known what happened to the chandeliers.

All that remains of the Riverside Inn is its 106-year-old lawn.

Magic Valley's Founding Fathers

By 1908, the Magic Valley was off to a good start.
Jerome County was still part of Lincoln County. Twin Falls County, however, had split from Cassia County. Twin Falls had grown from a village into a small city, and water from the Snake River was being diverted to farmland flanking the Snake River Canyon.
Clarence E. Bisbee gathered 14 of the valley's movers and shakers in his studio that year for a group portrait.
The Who's Who of the Magic Valley included:
• I.B. Perrine, who claimed the Snake River Canyon at Blue Lakes as his home in 1883 and is known as the father of the Magic Valley. Perrine orchestrated construction of the Milner, Oakley and Salmon Falls dams.
• Frank Gooding, born in Devon, England, the seventh governor of Idaho whose term ended in 1909. Gooding was elected to the U.S. Senate in 1920 and served until his death in 1928.
• Fentress Hill, of Twin Falls, an advisor to Gov. Gooding.
• State Sen. M.J. Sweeley, of Twin Falls. He persuaded the Legislature to create Shoshone Falls State Park. Sweeley was a member of the Trans-Mississippi Commercial Congress.

HIDDEN HISTORY

- Frank Buhl, a Sharon, Pa., steel magnate and philanthropist. Buhl was the largest investor in the Twin Falls Land and Water Co. and later was named president of the Twin Falls Southside Tract Project. His steel company, Sharon Iron Mills, manufactured the low-line siphon that carried canal water over Rock Creek.
- George Baird, of Twin Falls, vice president of the Twin Falls Southside Tract Project.
- J.H. Purdy, a director of the Twin Falls Oakley Land and Water Co.
- Fred Voight, of the Twin Falls Land and Water Co., was the first mayor of Twin Falls after the village became a second-class city in 1907.
- David MacWatters, vice president of Milner State Bank and board chairman of the Twin Falls North Side Land and Water Co.
- S.H. Hays, of the Twin Falls Land and Water Co. and a member of the National Irrigation Congress.
- A.C. Milner, of Salt Lake City, was an investor in the Twin Falls South Side Co.
- Harry Hollister, an agent of the Arnold Co. of Chicago, financed construction of the Shoshone Falls power plant. The plant began supplying electricity to Twin Falls in 1907.

PHOTO COURTESY OF CLARENCE E. BISBEE, TWIN FALLS COUNTY HISTORICAL MUSEUM

The Who's Who of 1908 Twin Falls included, standing, left to right: David MacWatters, Harry Hollister, M.J. Sweeley, Fentress Hill, S.H. Hill, Fred Voight, C.A. Tusch and R.F. Faris; and, bottom row, left to right: J.H. Purdy, A.C. Milner, Frank Gooding, George Baird, Frank Buhl, I.B. Perrine.

Mining on the Snake River

Gold was discovered in 1860 in what would become Idaho. Miners flocked to the area, and with them came more people. Freight-haulers kept the miners connected with suppliers on the outside, and storekeepers and cattlemen kept the miners fed.

The same scenario unfolded again and again across Idaho — even along the banks of the Snake River.

Gold was found below Shoshone Falls in 1869, and hundreds of miners moved into the canyon in hopes of finding their fortune.

The best mining was said to have been the stretch from just east of Murtaugh to Clark's Ferry, west of Twin Falls. In 1870, 400 men worked the sand bars in the canyon for $4 a day.

Three short-lived towns popped up in areas with the easiest access to the most gold flour: Shoshone City between Shoshone Falls and Twin Falls, Springtown near the present-day Hansen Bridge, and Drytown at the mouth of Dry Creek near Murtaugh.

Gold yields diminished quickly in the canyon, and many mining claims were sold or abandoned.

Miners began other careers, and business owners moved their operations out of the canyon as other settlements began to take shape.

PHOTO COURTESY OF C.R. SAVAGE, TWIN FALLS COUNTY HISTORICAL MUSEUM
A suspension bridge, built over the Snake River in 1902 for the Idaho Gold Mining Co., is seen in this C.R. Savage photograph.

HIDDEN HISTORY

The Home of Robert and Alice McCollum, Social Center

Robert McCollum and I.B. Perrine's friendship began in 1897, when McCollum was editor of the *Shoshone Journal.*
Perrine marketed produce from his Blue Lakes Ranch in front of the *Journal* building; McCollum's office was in the back.
Perrine talked his friend into being a partner in his fledgling irrigation project, then lost that support when he showed McCollum the site of the future Milner Dam.
The project was a crazy proposition, McCollum told Perrine.
McCollum soon changed his mind, however, and became secretary of Perrine's Twin Falls Investment Co. and, in 1904, built the first home in the new village of Twin Falls.
While the McCollums lived in what is known as a "stick-built" home, tents housed other residents, mostly young, single men or men who later would move their families to Twin Falls.
Alice McCollum took pity on these young "homeless" yet prominent men and invited them to join her family for dinner and socializing.
The group was known as the "Homeless Twenty," well after its membership tripled. The Homeless Twenty eventually became the Twin Falls Commercial Club, which evolved into the Chamber of Commerce.

PHOTO COURTESY OF CLARENCE E. BISBEE, TWIN FALLS COUNTY HISTORICAL MUSEUM
Robert and Alice McCollum's home was the first built in Twin Falls. Ann's Eyewear Boutique occupies the house today at Seventh Avenue North and Shoshone Street. The photo was taken from Seventh Avenue.

McCollum was a trustee of the village until Twin Falls became a town with a mayor-and-council government in 1907.

A 1944 Twin Falls High School publication described McCollum as "chief of police and rabbit catcher (and) was the entire population of Twin Falls."

The appearance of the McCollum house — now Ann's Eyewear Boutique on Shoshone Street North — has changed significantly over the past century, but the original front gables are still visible from Seventh Avenue North.

The Robert McCollum House Mix-up

A funny thing happened on the way to film a television program.

"Diggers," a history show on the National Geographic channel, was in town recently to document some metal-detector archeology at local historic sites. One of the sites is a property once owned by Twin Falls pioneer Robert M. McCollum, and is now listed on the Nation Register of Historic Places.

Local historian Jim Gentry was asked by "Diggers" producers to be at the McCollum house during the shoot, in case he was needed to identify anything found during the dig.

Gentry said he went to the property commonly known as the McCollum house — now the site of Ann's Eyewear Boutique, at the south corner of Shoshone Street and 7th Avenue North.

"I waited and waited, and no one showed up," Gentry said. Then he noticed a film crew working kitty corner from the McCollum house, at a Craftsman bungalow now owned by Twin Falls County.

"I walked up to the crew and asked them if they were looking for the McCollum house," Gentry said. "'It's over there,' I told them, and I pointed to Ann's Eyewear."

"Diggers" producers told Gentry that they had the correct location, and showed him the address listed on the National Register. That address belongs to the Craftsman bungalow at 708 E. Shoshone St., not Ann's Eyewear.

Gentry assumed it must be a mistake. Everyone knows that the McCollum home was the first home in Twin Falls – and that is Ann's Eyewear, he said.

A historical marker at the business identifies the building as the first framed, permanent residence built in Twin Falls.

The mistake, as it turns out, is the notion that there is only one McCollum home in Twin Falls.

The first home of Bob and Alice McCollum, on the corner of Shoshone Street and Seventh Avenue was indeed the first home in Twin Falls.

McCollum built a second home in 1910 for his daughter, Elva. The Craftsman

HIDDEN HISTORY

bungalow at 708 Shoshone St. E. is listed on the National Register.

Twin Falls' 1st Christmas Celebration

Where there are children, there must be a Christmas celebration — and a Christmas tree.

But in 1904, there were no pine trees to be found within 50 miles of the new town. Clumps of juniper could be seen growing in the foothills south of Twin Falls, so two young men volunteered to find the most beautiful juniper on the hillside for the community's first Christmas party.

Back in town, the absence of snow threatened the holiday spirit.

"Day after day, the children looked hopefully at the blue, unclouded sky," wrote local pioneer Anna Hansen Hayes. "Surely it would snow soon."

But the white flurries stirred by the cutting wind were simply flurries of dust that winter, Hayes said in a story written for the Idaho Territorial Centennial 50 years ago.

Enthusiasm ran high nonetheless, "perhaps to mask the homesickness which had threatened most of them in this dust-ridden land," she said.

Twin Falls was only a few months old. But by Christmas that year, nearly 100 children, school-aged and younger, lived within the town site. There was no formal school in town.

Local residents donated $600 for the construction of a one-room school house in September 1904. The Twin Falls Investment Co. donated two building lots for the school at the intersection of Idaho Street East and Third Avenue East. The school was built with donated labor, and was completed just in time for the Christmas party.

Paper ornaments and strings of popcorn and cranberries were prepared for the Christmas tree. One woman provided candles and a dozen glass ornaments from what must have seemed like a past life. And plans were made for Santa Claus to attend the party.

As promised, Sam Hamilton and Fred Eichoff headed out of town to cut down a juniper in the South Hills, fully expecting to be gone overnight. But they hadn't ridden far in their horse-drawn wagon when Hamilton spotted the perfect Christmas tree growing in a gully.

It was an 8-foot sagebrush.

Eichoff laughed at the suggestion, but Hamilton was out of his seat and had the sagebrush cut down before Eichoff had a chance to object.

The men knew they would be scolded by the women in town and ridiculed by the men. But somehow that sagebrush seemed more fitting than a juniper,

Hayes said.

That night, Hamilton and Eichoff sneaked back into town with the sagebrush and placed it in the new school house. After the jokes subsided the next morning, the women in town went to work on the tree.

The Christmas tree was stunning that year, Hayes said.

Twin Falls County Poor Farm

Caleb Lyon, Idaho territorial governor, signed Idaho's first indigence law, the "Act to Provide for the Better Maintenance of the Indigent Sick, Idiotic and Insane Persons, in the Several Counties of This Territory," in 1864. Funding to implement support for the needy was to come from property taxes and an annual per capita tax of $2. A special levy was to be placed into an account called the "Hospital Fund" and was to be controlled by county commissioners. Some counties used the cash to create farms where the poor could live and grow food.

DREW NASH, TIMES-NEWS
The old wall of the county poor farm still stands Wednesday, Sept. 3, 2014, near Twin Falls.

While other counties took advantage of evolving indigent laws, Twin Falls didn't need a poor farm until the Great Depression. The creation of a county poor farm was first suggested in 1931, but at that time, Twin Falls County was nearly broke.

The following year, charity was the city of Twin Falls' No. 1 expenditure, making up 41 percent of the city's budget, according to historian Jim Gentry.

Hundreds of homeless men camped in a two-mile section of Rock Creek locals called "jungletown."

An editorial column in the March 4, 1933 edition of the *Idaho Times* pleaded with local employers to hire local men: "Let's employ home labor."

While the newspaper supported

its eventual creation, "a poor farm should be the last step, for no community should take pride in such institutions or make it easy for indigents to avail themselves of the conveniences such an establishment provides," the editorial read.

A few months later, Commissioner Robert Rayl told the *Twin Falls Daily News* the county budget "has provided $8,000 for (the) site and $8,000 for building of a county poor farm."

That year, the county purchased land on 3700 North, east of the sugar factory. A hotel, which housed Amalgamated Sugar Co. employees, already sat on the property.

In 1940, the Works Projects Administration built the County Poor Farm, surrounded by a rock wall and distinctive arch way. Inside, residents raised their own food until grocers complained it competed with their business.

The county abandoned the poor farm in the late 1950s.

The sugar company, which now uses the rock enclosure for equipment storage, proclaimed the site's historical status and saved the rock walls and archway.

Twin Falls' First Jail

By the spring of 1905, Twin Falls' population had grown from three — John E. Hayes and his two-man survey crew in 1904 — to more than 500.

Nearly 200 men signed a petition to incorporate Twin Falls, and in April 1905, it became a village — two years before Twin Falls County was split from Cassia County.

The village was governed by a board of trustees, led by co-chairmen Paul Bickel and Sam Hamilton. Other trustees that year were Robert McCollum, Fred Eickhoff and F.D. Bradley.

Albert Snodgrass, village marshal, was the only paid official.

The board of trustees decided early that a jail was necessary, if only to house drunks.

Workers tunneled into the north bank of Rock Creek Canyon, south of today's Twin Falls Livestock Commission, to create a makeshift jail cell in the canyon's rock wall.

Only a few men, however, were held in the jail.

According to Hamilton, the jail door was intentionally left unlocked, in case prisoners needed to escape from a wandering rattlesnake.

"When word was passed around describing the jail and its probable reptile contents, wrongdoers avoided this section of the country, and the local crime rate took a decided decline," wrote Hamilton.

Later, the trustees learned that a federal law prohibited housing prisoners underground, and a new jail was built.

The new jail — completed in 1907 — was a 20-by-24 building at 240 Second Ave. S. It contained an office, a room with three steel cages and a separate room for female prisoners.

B-24 Crash on Mount Harrison

Only three peaks in southern Idaho rise above 9,000 feet: Cache Peak, at 10,339 feet; Mount Independence, 9,950 feet; and Mount Harrison, at 9,265 feet.

The peaks provide views of Utah and Nevada when the weather is clear. During winter though, the peaks, clustered in the Albion Range south of Burley, catch blizzards and many feet of snow.

In February 1945, Mount Harrison plucked an Army B-24 "Liberator" Bomber out of the sky, taking the lives of the nine men aboard.

The Liberator was flying to Mountain Home Air Force Base when it clipped the summit during a severe blizzard and quickly was covered by snow.

The crash site was spotted the next day by Lt. Harry Harris, flight B leader of

TIMES-NEWS FILE PHOTO
A fire lookout is seen on the summit of Mount Harrison, above the site of a 1945 B-24 bomber crash.

the Twin Falls Civil Air Patrol, but blizzard conditions hampered recovery efforts for more than a week.

An Army ground crew came within several miles of the wreckage but couldn't get closer in the bad weather and deep snow. Army equipment foundered in the drifts, and the crew had to spend the night in a ranger's cabin before returning to Burley.

Then-Cassia County Sheriff Saul Clark recruited a group of experienced mountaineers several days later, but weather prevented their departure.

More than a week after the crash, the search party plowed through the snow on horseback to reach the wreckage near Horse Thief Lake, 200 feet below the summit.

The group recovered the bodies of the men and carried them off the mountain. The Army removed all traces of the crash after the snow melted the following summer.

Nearly 60 years later, Almo resident and history buff Arlo Lloyd and several descendants of the men killed honored the crew with a memorial plaque overlooking the crash site, just east of the Mount Harrison lookout.

Crew members killed in the crash were 2nd Lt. Clinton R. Madeley, of New Jersey; 2nd Lt. James P. Sanders, of Alabama; Flight Officer Frank J. Pryor, of Georgia; Flight Officer Stuart McMaster, of New York; Sgt. Don McClure, of Kentucky; Cpl. William Doyle, of Michigan; Cpl. William J. Little, of Pennsylvania; Cpl. Charles Tucker, of Kansas; and Cpl. George Ellet, of New York.

Location of Twin Falls Train Depot Carefully Contemplated

The location of the town's train depot can't be found on any map today. That's because the streets' names have changed twice since the townsite was platted.

William Ashton, chief engineer of the Oregon Short Line, announced plans for the depot in May 1905, according to the *Twin Falls Weekly News*.

The railway grade was at the edge of town, and the side tracks and train station were to be graded next, Ashton said.

The depot would be built "a half a block west of Shoshone Avenue, between Shoshone Avenue and Ninth Street," the newspaper said. That's across Minidoka Avenue from the Depot Grill and a half block off Shoshone Street today.

"It will be so located as to facilitate traffic and prevent the blocking of the streets by train," the newspaper said.

MYCHEL MATTHEWS

PHOTO COURTESY OF CLARENCE E. BISBEE, TWIN FALLS COUNTY HISTORICAL MUSEUM
The Oregon Short Line depot is seen in this early C.E. Bisbee photo. Plans to build the depot were announced in May 1905.

At the time, Shoshone Avenue ended at Rock Creek, but the same article informed readers that "a viaduct will soon span the stream on the thoroughfare." "The traffic into Twin Falls by this avenue promises to be very heavy as the country to the immediate west is already thickly settled," the article continued, promising that "the avenue will be graded and leveled, making it a magnificent highway."

Ashton predicted that the railroad would be finished by July 1, 1905.

Addison T. Smith

Yes, that Addison.
The avenue that bears the name of Twin Falls lawyer and U.S. Rep. Addison T. Smith is an obvious clue that Smith claimed Twin Falls as his home. Less obvious clues are the Addison T. Smith building on Shoshone Street South and the Addison T. Smith subdivision northeast of North 5 Points.
Smith began his political career in 1891 in Washington, D.C., as secretary to Republican U.S. Sen. George L. Shoup of Idaho. He later joined the staff of U.S. Sen. Weldon B. Heyburn, another Idaho Republican.
While in Boise in 1902, Smith met Bob McCollum, editor of the *Shoshone Journal* and a friend of Twin Falls founder I.B. Perrine.
In early 1904, McCollum wrote to Smith, telling him of the poor turnout for the first land drawing in Twin Falls. Only 25 applicants showed for the drawing, he said.
Later that year, McCollum invited Smith to Twin Falls to see the work being done to dam the Snake River at Milner.

HIDDEN HISTORY

PHOTO COURTESY OF CLARENCE E. BISBEE, TWIN FALLS COUNTY HISTORICAL MUSEUM
Addison T. Smith, right, shakes the hand of 97-year-old Civil War veteran and Twin Falls pioneer Horace Hart on July 20, 1927.

Smith was impressed — so impressed, he asked McCollum to find him 160 acres to buy near Twin Falls. Within weeks, McCollum notified Smith that he had found an irrigated parcel adjacent to the city.

Smith was one of 90 Republicans who voted in Twin Falls' first election in November 1904, his memoirs say. Three residents voted the Democratic ticket.

Smith was appointed registrar of the U.S. Land Office in Boise in 1907. The success of the Twin Falls Tract is partially credited to Smith's constant promotion of the area.

He continued to serve on Heyburn's staff until Heyburn's death in 1912.

In 1913, Smith was elected to the U.S. House, representing Idaho's 2nd District until 1933.

Although Smith lived in Washington most of his life, he claimed Twin Falls as his residence and voted under the absentee law until his death in 1956.

DREW NASH, TIMES-NEWS
Addison T. Smith's name is seen Wednesday, Aug. 13, 2014, on what used to be Smith's law building, constructed in 1910 on Shoshone Street South.

MYCHEL MATTHEWS

Twin Falls Golf Club

In 1931, a nine-hole golf course was constructed west of Rock Creek in Twin Falls, smack dab on top of what had been the Old Oregon Trail.

The trail followed the east bank of Rock Creek from Stricker Ranch south of Hansen, then crossed the creek near today's Amalgamated Sugar Co.'s plant. Swales of the Oregon Trail are still visible on the golf course as the trail headed north toward the Snake River.

Steve Meyerhoeffer, a golf professional at the club, said the ninth fairway has two swales running from south to north that are consistent with where the trail would have run along Rock Creek.

The golf course was originally a private club, said Dennis Bowyer, director of Twin Falls City Parks and Recreation Department.

"It wasn't a city course until 1939, when the private club donated it to the city," Bowyer said. As a stipulation of the deed, former members of the private club were able to golf for free at the club for 10 years after the donation.

Sometime in the 1960s, the city expanded the course into 18 holes.

Former Twin Falls Mayor Gale Kleinkoph has played the golf course for decades. "Golf definitely gets in your blood," he said.

As evidence, Kleinkoph cited golf's Hiskey family, formerly of Twin Falls. Pete Hiskey, a former director of the city parks department and superintendent of the course, helped build the original nine-hole course, and his sons, Jim, Babe and Sonny, grew up in a rock house near the fourth green, Meyerhoeffer said.

The three sons won eight consecutive Idaho amateur championships and multiple NCAA trophies among them. Babe Hiskey, who was the only golfer named as one of Idaho's top 50 athletes by *Sports Illustrated*, beat Jack Nicklaus and Arnold Palmer to win the Cajun Classic, and would later appear in two Masters championships.

The name of the course has evolved over the years, from the Twin Falls Country Club to the Twin Falls Municipal Golf Course, to the Twin Falls Golf Club. But it's OK to refer to it as "the Muni," says the city's website.

MYCHEL MATTHEWS, TIMES-NEWS
Golfers unknowingly cross the Old Oregon Trail Wednesday as they head to Hole No. 9 at the Twin Falls Golf Club.

Fair Times

Fairs have long been a popular recreation in the Magic Valley. The first fair was a Halloween Festival held in 1905 at the north corner of Shoshone Street and Second Avenue North. I.B. Perrine displayed gold medals he won for his fruit earlier that year at the World Fair in Portland, Ore.

PHOTO COURTESY OF CLARENCE E. BISBEE, TWIN FALLS COUNTY HISTORICAL MUSEUM

Fair-goers are seen at the newly built fairgrounds in Filer.

Small fairs were later held at local schools — in 1912 at Washington School west of Filer and in 1913 at the Union School at Curry.

In 1915, James McMillan, secretary of the Twin Falls Commercial Club, pitched the idea of a permanent county fair.

Filer businessmen supported the idea and purchased 40 acres on the east side of town, then turned the parcel over to the county.

The first fair was held at the new fairgrounds in 1916. During the Great Depression, Twin Falls County was broke and couldn't afford to hold a fair, which put the county at risk of losing the fairgrounds to its original owners.

But county youngsters came to the rescue by holding 4-H and FFA Fairs in 1932, 1933 and 1934.

PHOTO COURTESY OF CLARENCE E. BISBEE, TWIN FALLS COUNTY HISTORICAL MUSEUM

The first fair was a Halloween Festival held in 1905 at the north corner of Shoshone Street and Second Avenue North. The first fair at the Filer fairgrounds was in 1916.

The Day the River Went Dry

PHOTO COURTESY OF CLARENCE E. BISBEE, TWIN FALLS COUNTY HISTORICAL MUSEUM
Men are seen closing the head gates into the Main Canal prior to filling the Milner Dam. The date on the photo is incorrect. The correct date is March 1, 1905.

On March 1, 1905, the gates of the newly completed Milner Dam were closed for the first time.
And for the first time, the Snake River went dry, as river water backed up nearly to Burley.
The town of Milner — now defunct — sprang up during the construction of the dam.
The dam raised the river 38 feet — enough to push water into the Twin Falls Canal Co.'s main canal on the south side of the Snake River.
The following day, water from the reservoir was diverted into the canal system to fill Murtaugh Lake, then turned loose to irrigate thousands of acres of land in the Magic Valley.

'Ee Dah How' Not the Origin of Idaho

Generations of Idahoans grew up thinking the state's name came from an Indian word meaning "The Sun Comes over the Mountains."
The "Ee Dah How" fable continued for decades in fourth-grade Idaho History textbooks.
Now textbooks "introduce (the 'Ee Dah How' story) as a tale, and then give the real fact for how our state was named," said Lori Hinton, who teaches fourth grade and Idaho History at Morningside Elementary School in Twin Falls.
When the U.S. House voted to create a new territory in 1863, its name was to be "Montana," according to historian Carlos Schwantes. But several senators didn't like the name.
"Montana is no name at all," proclaimed Sen. Henry Wilson of Massachusetts,

HIDDEN HISTORY

says Schwantes' book "In Mountain Shadows, A History of Idaho."
Oregon Sen. Franklin Harding agreed and proposed "Idaho" instead.
"Idaho, in English, signifies 'Gem of the Mountains,'" said Harding, referring to a story told by the owner of a steamboat named "Idaho" that taxied gold miners up the Columbia River.
The boat owner had heard the name from a miner who said it was an Indian word proposed for the new territory of Colorado.
Lobbyist George M. Willing suggested the name "Idaho" to Congress when the Colorado Territory was first organized, claiming it was a Shoshone word for "the sun comes from the mountains," Schwantes said.
Some say Idaho Springs, Colo., took its name during the debate over Colorado's name.
Later, Willing admitted he invented the word "Idaho" and had made up the whole story about it being an Indian word, Schwantes said.
Contacted by phone Wednesday, Sandy (Smith) Bronson, a city employee of Idaho Springs, said she couldn't confirm the story because she hadn't lived in Idaho Springs that long.
Turns out, Bronson was born and raised in Twin Falls.

The Albion Normal School: Training Students to be Teachers

PHOTO COURTESY OF CLARENCE E. BISBEE, TWIN FALLS COUNTY HISTORICAL MUSEUM
In its prime, the Albion State Normal School trained most schoolteachers in southern Idaho.

The Albion State Normal School was one of only two teaching colleges in early Idaho.
Three years after Idaho became a state, Albion residents lobbied to get the school built in town. Albion then was the Cassia County seat and the center of population in south-central Idaho.
In 1893, state Sen. J.E. Miller donated 5 acres for the campus, and townsfolk built the school themselves.
Girls needed to be 14, and boys 15, to take preparatory classes at the college.
The "normal" course consisted of one to three years of training to teach or four years to earn a lifetime certificate.

The school's athletic teams were known as the "Teachers" until 1935, when they became the "Panthers." School colors were red and black, and the student yearbook was called "The Sage."

In 1947, the school was renamed "Southern Idaho College of Education" and authorized to grant baccalaureate degrees.

After the school had graduated about 6,000 students, Gov. Len B. Jordan closed it in 1951.

The Albion campus was listed on the National Register of Historic Places in 1980.

Roseworth: A Failed Settlement

Nearly two decades after the creation of the Twin Falls irrigation system, a caravan of folks from Brooklyn, N.Y., traveled to Idaho to settle an area 10 miles south of Castleford and 20 miles west of Hollister. According to a 1921 article in *Motor Life Magazine*, the band of travelers was "a group of good, substantial American citizens, tired of the strain and the noise of city life, who are eager to begin anew on the land."

The group — organized by William D. Scott and called "Scott's Modern Caravan" — was the first large migration west in automobiles and was under the supervision of the American Automobile Association, the magazine wrote.

GUS KELKER, TIMES-NEWS

A large crane is seen in this 1964 photo during the construction of the Roseworth flume in the desert landscape near Roseworth.

"Instead of the rather uncomfortable ... prairie schooners, these 1921 pioneers will ride in the latest model touring-car, equipped with a camp bungalow trailer really luxuriously fitted with electricity, beds and mattresses, gasoline-burning cook stoves, and every modern convenience," the magazine said. Instead of traveling 12 miles a day, as earlier pioneers traveled with an ox-drawn cart, these pioneers traveled "at a sensible, steady 12 mph pace (to) soon bring the caravan to its destination."

About 200 people, traveling in 42 automobiles, made the 3,400-mile trip from Brooklyn to the desert landscape of Roseworth.

Few of the settlers were experienced farmers, and none had experience irrigating farm ground. So when the caravan arrived in southern Idaho's

GUS KELKER, TIMES-NEWS
The large funnel of the Roseworth flume stretches through the desert landscape to carry irrigation water to farm ground near Roseworth. A dirt road for vehicles runs parallel to the flume.

desert, most were bitterly disappointed and felt they had been duped, wrote Jim Gentry in his book "In the Middle and on the Edge."
All but three of the settlers returned back East in less than two years. Those who stayed moved to Twin Falls.
Years later, the land got a boost from irrigation water out of Cedar Creek.
The Roseworth flume, which transported water to the Roseworth Tract, was constructed in 1964.
The Roseworth area was first settled by cattlemen in the 1890s, and named for Rose Worth, a daughter of one of the pioneers.

Al Faussett Shoots the Falls

Al Faussett was a cocky sort.
"Al was always betting and wild and into something new," said his great-grandson Guy Faussett. "He always had some new scheme... because he was going to get rich somehow."

The well-to-do Faussett family settled in Monroe, Wash., at the end of the 19th century. Al Faussett was always looking for attention.

The early 20th century was a time when daredevils took on crazy challenges, such as doing stunts on the wings of biplanes or going over Niagara Falls in a barrel.

In 1926, Fox Studios offered $1,500 to anyone who tried to run Sunset Falls on the North Fork of the Skykomish River in Washington in a canoe.

A lumberjack by trade, Faussett carved a 34-foot canoe from a spruce log, but Fox rejected the watercraft because it was not a replica of an Indian canoe.

Instead, Faussett charged $1 admission to see the stunt. He went over 104-foot Sunset Falls in his canoe and emerged unscathed and $3,000 richer.

During the next few years, Faussett ran five more falls, suffering only a concussion and two broken ribs. He then set his sights on 212-foot Shoshone Falls.

On July 28, 1929, an audience of 5,000 spectators — including a Fox film crew — gathered at the falls to watch as Faussett maneuvered his canvas-covered football-shaped canoe into place.

After fitting himself into the canoe, he stuffed inner tubes into the cockpit for

PHOTO COURTESY OF C.E. BISBEE, TWIN FALLS COUNTY HISTORICAL MUSEUM
Monroe, Wash., daredevil Al Faussett canoed over Shoshone Falls in 1929 and shared the proceeds from the event with the Twin Falls post of the American Legion.

cushioning and zipped the canvas hatch closed.

Faussett wanted to steer the canoe over the south edge of the falls — which is usually dry during irrigation season — so Idaho Power Co. increased the flow over the falls to accommodate him.

Faussett hedged his bet by running a thin wire from a large boulder upstream, through a 3-inch ring on the bow of his canoe and to a boat below the falls. After launching from the south side of the river, the canoe snagged at the brink. Two men waded into the river with poles and gave the canoe a push, sending it over the falls.

The event earned Faussett $1,466, half of which he gave to the Twin Falls Post of the American Legion.

Early Twin Falls a Lonely Place

In the oldest section of the Twin Falls Cemetery, unmarked graves testify to the lonely existence lived by early settlers.

No headstone adorns Peter A. Johnson's grave, and only a vague description of its location is known.

Johnson's is one among many unmarked graves in the cemetery, dated between 1906 and 1918, said cemetery owner Rick Muse.

The Sept. 17, 1909, headline in the *Twin Falls Weekly News* said Johnson "died unattended in a lonely shack" a mile east of Twin Falls. In 1909, that meant somewhere along Eastland Drive.

Dr. H.W. Clouchek and county Coroner C. J. Walker first assumed Johnson was a victim of foul play. But after examining the body, they found no evidence to support the theory.

Still, no cause of death ever was determined. Johnson was in good physical condition when he died.

Johnson was last seen alive by his employee, Florenco Funk, on Sept. 11, 1909. Funk found Johnson's body two days later in the shack they shared on the M. A Stronk farm east of town.

Johnson worked a portion of Stronk's farm for shares.

He had recently paid $500 for a building lot in Twin Falls. Johnson owned four horses, a wagon and a mowing machine, which indicated to the coroner that he was "of an industrious, frugal temperament," according to the article.

Walker said he believed Johnson had left money cached somewhere, though none was ever found.

Funk testified that Johnson "had been complaining recently, and seemed to be suffering from mental depression for some time," the article said.

PHOTO COURTESY OF CLARENCE E. BISBEE, TWIN FALLS COUNTY HISTORICAL MUSEUM
Looking east on an early Twin Falls County road.

Johnson had no family in town, but Walker found papers that showed he had a son, Carl Harold Johnson.

He also found many letters from Johnson's ex-wife. The letters were about four years old and were written in Swedish.

Clouchek and Walker concluded that Johnson died of "acute dilation of the heart," the article said.

Johnson was "given a respectable burial" in the Twin Falls Cemetery after no one claimed his remains.

John Hansen, Busy Pioneer

In 1889, the first recorded water war occurred in the Magic Valley.

John Hansen, who had moved to southern Idaho more than a decade before, taught school at the Oakley Meadows stage station on the northeast edge of the South Hills.

Hansen, who was born in Denmark, farmed and raised livestock along Cottonwood Creek, which meandered out of Cottonwood Canyon near Oakley

HIDDEN HISTORY

to merge with Dry Creek at Lake Linden.

Lake Linden was later expanded into a reservoir for the south side canal system and became known as Murtaugh Lake.

John Caldwell lived upstream from Hansen on Cottonwood Creek and raised his own crops and livestock.

Apparently, Caldwell was not content with sharing the creek with his neighbor and he dammed the creek, completely cutting off Hansen's water.

When Hansen realized his water had been captured upstream, he tore out Caldwell's dam.

Caldwell filed charges against Hansen at Albion, then the seat of Cassia County, and Hansen was arrested.

But the charges backfired on Caldwell.

MYCHEL MATTHEWS, TIMES-NEWS
John Hansen's headstone is seen at the Rock Creek Cemetery south of Hansen. City founders promised Hansen they would name the town after him if he moved his mercantile from Rock Creek to the new town on the rail road 7 miles north.

The judge sided with Hansen and appointed him water master on the Goose Creek drainage, north of Oakley. Hansen, alongside Cassia County Surveyor Frank Riblett, had years of experience studying the lay of the land south of the Snake River and, in 1891, filed a claim for water at the Cedars, near today's Milner Dam. Hansen and Riblett calculated that 300,000 acres could be irrigated from water diverted from the river.

Hansen was elected probate judge in 1892 and Cassia County clerk in 1894.

In 1900, Hansen moved to the town of Rock Creek, where he opened a store. A few years later, I.B. Perrine took Hansen and Riblett's idea and created the Twin Falls Irrigation Tract.

Soon, the railroad entered the area along the south side of the Snake River. A new townsite was being surveyed along the railroad, seven miles east of Twin Falls. Investors offered to name the town after Hansen if he would relocate his store from Rock Creek to the new town.

In 1907, John Hansen was appointed as a county commissioner when Twin Falls County was created from the west end of Cassia County.

Nat-Soo-Pah Becomes a Tourist Attraction

A swath of artesian hot springs lies at the base of the South Hills south of Twin Falls.
Several natatoria — indoor swimming pools equivalent to today's health spa — cropped up over the years within that geothermal zone.
For decades, folks hauled water from one of the springs, near Wild Horse Springs east of Hollister, before the springs became a tourist attraction.
In 1930, the Hot Wells Development Co. opened a natatorium at the springs and a contest was held to name the new resort.
The name "Wild Rose Pool and Playground," submitted by Julia Kunkle of nearby Amsterdam, won second place, while "Nat-Soo-Pah" took the prize.
Vernon Mund, a Twin Falls man who was attending Princeton at the time, submitted the name, explaining Nat-Soo-Pah meant "the water which now bubbles into and fills the new plunge," according to a 1989 *Times-News* article written by local historian Virgina Ricketts.
But the owners of the spa took the name and embellished the story, Ricketts said.

PHOTO COURTESY OF CLARENCE E. BISBEE, TWIN FALLS COUNTY HISTORICAL MUSEUM
Nat-Soo-Pah Natatorium, east of Hollister, is seen shortly after opening in 1930.

An August 1930, *Idaho Evening Times* article said the owners claimed Nat-Soo-Pah supposedly means "a special gift from the Great spirit as being healing or health waters" — a title more appealing to tourists.
According to a sign at the early spa, Nat-Soo-Pah's "'Magic Mineral Water' comes through a layer of iron pyrite 'fool's gold' which gives the water in the swimming pool a greenish color."

Jack Rabbits, Scourge of the Past

Imagine being a rabbit in 1904 Twin Falls, with little to eat but sagebrush.
No water, no farms, no food.

HIDDEN HISTORY

PHOTO COURTESY OF CLARENCE E. BISBEE, TWIN FALLS COUNTY HISTORICAL MUSEUM
A large jack rabbit population could destroy a farmer's entire crop in no time. This rabbit drive took place in Jerome County in 1913.

Then came irrigation. Suddenly a rabbit's life became much easier, with rows and rows of crops and the tender bark of young fruit trees to feast on.

The Twin Falls canal system first delivered water to farms in 1905. It didn't take long for the rabbit population to explode.

Rabbits quickly become a major threat to the success of the new irrigation tract and rabbit drives became the solution.

In 1906, 12,000 of the critters were rounded up and killed by 40 men, woman and children in a single rabbit drive.

Over the years, thousands more met their fate at the end of a club.

Barrymore: Almost a Town

Dry land north of the Snake River waited several years for irrigation water after Milner dam was constructed.

One thousand people showed up in April 1907 for the first land drawing in Jerome County, a year before water was directed into the north-side canal system, according to the 75th anniversary edition of the *North Side News*, published in 1982.

The largest land drawing in the county was held six months later in what would become the city of Jerome.
Less than three years later, county residents proposed a new town on Dr. Leininger's property three miles southeast of Jerome.
The town was to be named "Manson," but within a few months Manson became known as "Jonathan," at least on paper.
Promoters of the new town made little headway until the Rupert-Bliss branch of the Oregon Short Line railroad was completed and a community hall was built on land donated by Dr. Leininger.
As the community began to gel, locals again changed the name to "Barrymore" after the popular actress Ethel Barrymore, sister of actors John and Lionel Barrymore.
Barrymore — who would later be known as the great-aunt of today's actress Drew Barrymore — was then known as "the First Lady of American Theater."
The Barrymore Improvement Association was formed in 1912 to promote the proposed town. When Barrymore Hall was completed the following year, the Barrymore Civic Club formed and took over the promotion.
Under a private contract, George Epperson hauled children from the area to Jerome schools until the Jerome School District built a school house in Barrymore. Estelle Mauldin Ricketts was the first teacher.
Barrymore Union Church was soon built across the street from the school and the Barrymore post office quickly followed. In 1914, Ernest Witt became the first and last postmaster of Barrymore.
The closing of the post office in 1916 struck the first blow to the young community. In 1919, Canyonside Church purchased and moved the Barrymore Union church building.
Barrymore School closed in 1924 and the building was moved across the street. Barrymore Hall stood until 1945, when the Barrymore Civic Club sold the building. The land that had been donated for the hall was returned to farm ground, as dictated by the terms of the donation.
Barrymore — which never incorporated — was located on Barrymore Road, one mile west of U.S. 93.

May Day, a Celebration

Early settlers celebrated May 1, or May Day, by dancing and weaving ribbons around a maypole.
The May Day tradition began as a way to celebrate the end of long, cold winters and the coming of summerlike weather.

HIDDEN HISTORY

CLARENCE E. BISBEE PHOTOS COURTESY OF TWIN FALLS COUNTY HISTORICAL MUSEUM
These undated C. E. Bisbee photos were taken in the Twin Falls City Park during the town's first May Day celebration about 1910.

The Need for Speed

In June 1909, the Alaska-Yukon-Pacific Exposition was held in Seattle. President William Howard Taft officially opened the expo at 3 p.m. June 1. At the same moment, five cars left the starting line of the transcontinental auto race at City Hall in New York City.

The race — known formally as the "Transcontinental Contest for the Guggenheim Trophy" — ended 22 days later in Seattle.

Sponsors Robert Guggenheim, the AYP Expo, the Seattle Automobile Club, the Automobile Club of America and Henry Ford, who entered two cars in the contest, hoped the race would focus attention on the need for new and improved roads across America.

Roads were so bad back then that 29 automakers backed out of the race, leaving only Ford's two Model Ts, a 1908 Shawmut, a 60-horsepower Itala, a six-cylinder Acme and a Model 30-60 Stearns, which started two days late and never left New York state.

The drivers had to pass through 30 towns between New York and Seattle, picking up "passports" to prove they had driven through each town, including Pocatello, Twin Falls and Boise.

One of the Model Ts was the first to arrive in Seattle on June 23, 1909, winning the Guggenheim trophy and a $2,000 prize. The Shawmut arrived several hours later. Ford's other car arrived third, after being held up for seven hours on Washington's Snoqualmie Pass.

Ford quickly used his win to promote his car company. But after the expo closed, his winning car was disqualified because its drivers had replaced its

engine during the race.
The Shawmut eventually was declared the winner.

M.B. MARTIN, PUBLIC DOMAIN
This 1908 Shawmut finished second in the 1909 'Transcontinental Contest for the Guggenheim Trophy' but was declared the winner by default several months later. The car is seen in front of the Hotel Perrine in Twin Falls during the race.

Farm Labor Camps in WWII

President Franklin D. Roosevelt signed in 1942 an order placing people of Japanese ancestry into 11 relocation centers throughout the West.
Jerome County's Hunt Camp, known now as the Minidoka Relocation Center at the Minidoka National Historic Site, was the largest center and housed 9,000 people during World War II.
Between 1942 and 1944, 33,000 Japanese-Americans volunteered to leave the relocation centers to work on farms and lived with their families in farm labor camps operated by the Farm Security Administration, according to the Oregon Cultural Heritage Commission.
Large numbers of these evacuees were housed in two labor camps in the Magic Valley. Residents at each camp elected council members to govern within the general regulations of the FSA.
At Twin Falls, the FSA housed Japanese-Americans at a pre-WWII farm labor camp south of town.
The Rupert camp was a former Civilian Conservation Corps camp.

HIDDEN HISTORY

In the summer of 1942, FSA photographer Russell Lee documented life at the labor camps. The Oregon Cultural Heritage Commission produced "Uprooted: Japanese-American Farm Labor Camps during World War II," a traveling photography exhibition, which features Lee's work.

PHOTO COURTESY OF RUSSELL LEE, U.S. NATIONAL PARK SERVICE
The National Park Service is working on a new project to reconstruct one of the 1940s ball field from the Minidoka camp, known locally as Hunt Camp. The park service is looking for photographs and stories from the camp that may help the project. Seen in this NPS photo are two Japanese Americans from the Hunt Camp taking down the flag at a farm labor camp in the Magic Valley.

Horse Thieves and Escaped Bears at Devils Corral

Lions and tigers and bears. Oh, my. No one knows who named Devils Corral, a rugged canyon area on the north side of the Snake River between the Twin Falls and Shoshone Falls. But the name appears on an 1879 U.S. Corps of Engineers map.

The area was well known as a hangout for horse thieves who roamed southern Idaho in the 1870s and 1880s.

In 1907, Alpha Kinsey bought the lower corral area from the Mabbutt family of Jerome County, then filed

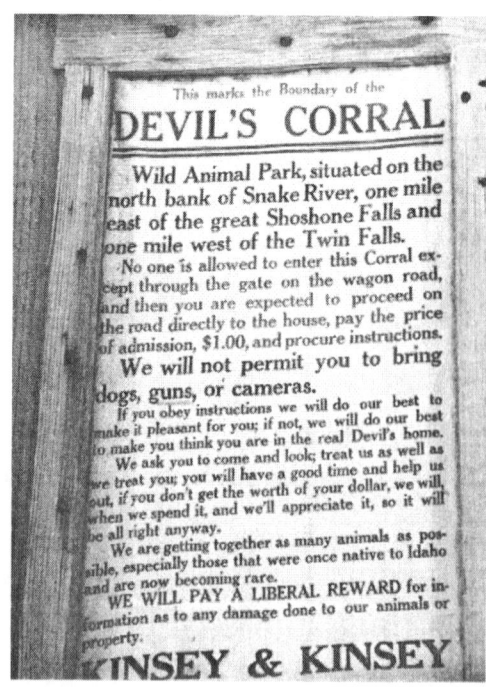

PHOTO COURTESY OF CLARENCE E. BISBEE, TWIN FALLS COUNTY HISTORICAL MUSEUM
Brothers Alpha and Harry Kinsey operated a zoo for wild circus animals in Devils Corral.

a homestead claim on adjacent property.

Kinsey and his brother, Harry, moved their families to the corral and opened a wildlife park. Promotional material claimed the park held "circus animals." Kinsey purchased a small herd of deer for the park, followed by a couple of bears and a pair of blue heron. Kinsey hoped to add mountain sheep and goats to the park.

In 1917, Kinsey started a fish hatchery at the corral.

The Kinseys eventually abandoned the Wild Animal Park because the animals kept escaping.

One of the escaped bears was found in a grain field on the south side of the canyon. The bear was dragging a chain and was tame, according to a newspaper account.

An Eden family adopted the bear, but after a time, had the bear butchered. The fate of the second bear and other animals is not known.

Harmon Park: a Gift to the Community

William E. Harmon was a self-made real estate magnate, born in Lebanon, Ohio, in 1862.

Harmon started his fortune by buying blocks of Cincinnati property to subdivide and sell to potential homeowners. He sold the building lots for a tiny down payment — $1 — followed by monthly installments.

His idea revolutionized real estate marketing by making the dream of homeownership achievable for average families.

Harmon is best known for his philanthropic efforts, especially his endowments promoting artistic and scientific achievements in the African-American community.

He believed that all a person needed was a small gift and a bit of encouragement. Some of these gifts came in the form of checks signed by "Jedidiah Tingle," which was the name of Harmon's great-grandfather.

A letter accompanied the checks, explaining that the money was sent "to bring smiles and tender thoughts to the great in heart in high and low places, to comfort and cheer those who do exceptional things, or (who) suffer."

Harmon's identity as the donor was not disclosed until after his death in 1928. In 1922, he created the Harmon Foundation to carry out his humanitarian efforts. In 1924, the foundation granted money to 100 small towns across the country to purchase land for community parks.

The young town of Twin Falls received $2,000 from the foundation that year to build a Harmon Park at Elizabeth Boulevard and Locust Street.

HIDDEN HISTORY

PHOTO COURTESY OF STEVE WOODALL
The Harmon Park swimming pool is seen in this undated photo.

Numerous civic organizations raised money for a swimming pool at Harmon Park. The pool was constructed in the 1930s with local labor provided by the federal Works Projects Administration.

The Junior Chamber of Commerce — or Jaycees — in 1939 built a baseball park, Jaycee Field, north of the pool.

The swimming pool closed in 1948, and a new pool was built in 1949 to the east of the old pool — where the Twin Falls Skateboard Park is today.

The Rise of Moving Pictures in Twin Falls

Early residents liked to be entertained, and the result was a proliferation of silver screens in Twin Falls.

Movie houses "are fast becoming almost as numerous as cigar stores or confectionary stands in every part of the country," the Twin Falls News reported in 1907.

The city's first theater opened in 1907 above the Mission Cafe on Main Avenue North, across the street from the Hotel Perrine.

Owners P.W. Alexander and C.W. Tschumy, both of Ohio, held a contest to name the theater, and Mary Milner won $5 in gold for suggesting the "Majestic."

The Majestic was sold the next year and moved to 130 Main Ave. S. in what had been the Stothard Hardware Co.

It reopened in 1908 as the Dime Theater. The new owners were smart to re-engage the popular Miss Fargo, pianist, and Miss McCrait, soloist, the Twin Falls News opined.

The same year, one of the owners of the Dime Theater opened the Iris Moving Picture Theater at 325 Shoshone St. S. with "an audience that bulged out onto the sidewalk ..."

By 1910, the town had plans for a $150,000 opera house on Second Avenue West behind the Perrine Hotel.

It never materialized, but several years later, the smaller Lavering Opera House opened on Second Avenue East — known as the "Blacker's Furniture" building today. The Lavering was the first of many to double as a vaudeville theater and movie house.

The first block of Shoshone Street North became known as "Theater Row."

After the Isis, the 350-seat Orsis Theater was built on the west corner of Shoshone and Second Avenue North, followed by the Luna, the Grand, the Revier and the Rialto theaters.

The Orpheum — considered the granddaddy of Twin Falls theaters — opened in 1906 on Main Street South. It moved to Theater Row, then moved around the corner to its present location in 1918.

PHOTO COURTESY OF CLARENCE E. BISBEE, TWIN FALLS COUNTY HISTORICAL MUSEUM
The Realto Theater, at 131 Shoshone St. N., is seen in this C.E. Bisbee photo.

The Rogerson Hotel was Early Elegance in Twin Falls

In the mid-1880s, a wool shortage predicted to last a decade brought sheepmen to southern Idaho, where the bunchgrass range was considered ideal for raising the woolly critters.

Robert Rogerson, a Scottish sheepman from Iowa, settled in Idaho Territory in 1887 in Deep Creek Meadows, about 20 miles north of the Nevada line. Brother Andy joined him in 1889.

In 1908, Rogerson built a grand hotel on the north corner of Main Avenue and Hansen Street East in Twin Falls. Designed by well-known architect C. Harvey Smith, who also designed the Twin Falls County Courthouse, the hotel was to have had six stories. Only three floors were built, though, at a cost of $70,000. The first floor housed businesses, including the Lobby Cigar Store, a popular headquarters for baseball fans, and the Meyer and Co.'s Head to Foot Outfitters. The second and third floors were occupied by the Rogerson European Hotel office, lobby, public and private baths and 96 bedrooms.

HIDDEN HISTORY

PHOTO COURTESY OF CLARENCE E. BISBEE, TWIN FALLS COUNTY HISTORICAL MUSEUM
The lobby of the Rogerson European Hotel is seen in this early C.E. Bisbee photograph. The three-story hotel was built in 1908. The third floor was destroyed by fire in 1965.

The dining room boasted fine silver, china and linens, and an orchestra for diners' entertainment.

In 1909, railroad officials changed the name of Deep Creek Meadows to "Terminal City" because the branch line from Twin Falls ended there.

Rogerson platted a townsite on his property next to the terminal depot. The town became known as Rogerson but never was incorporated.

Rogerson and his wife moved in 1920 to Phoenix. He died there in 1938 and was buried in the Twin Falls Cemetery.

The building is scheduled for demolition but still stands at the north corner of Main Avenue and Hansen Street East.

Remember the Maine

In mid-January 1898, President William McKinley ordered the USS Maine to Havana as a symbol of U.S. support of Cuban independence from Spain. A month later, the ship exploded in the harbor, killing 266 of the 355 men aboard.

Although Spain denied any connection to the explosion, the U.S. Navy disagreed. Many Americans took up the cry, "Remember the Maine! To hell with Spain!"

In March, the Navy concluded that a mine had destroyed the ship. The following month, McKinley asked Congress to send troops to the harbor and 10 days later ordered a blockade of Cuba.

Spain declared war on the U.S., which reciprocated. The Spanish-American War lasted only a few months. The treaty called for Spain to grant Cuba its independence and to turn over the Philippines, Puerto Rico and Guam to the U.S.

A decade later, much mystery still surrounded the explosion. The Maine was raised in 1912 and closely examined, but the conclusion was the same: A mine caused the explosion, the Navy said.

Spain, however, was eventually cleared of all responsibility for the explosion that destroyed the battleship.

In 1913, artist Charles Keck sculpted a plaque commemorating the lives lost on the ship and more than a thousand casts were made from bronze salvaged from the wreckage.

It is said that each of the 89 survivors, as well as the families of the men that died, received a memorial plaque, while others were spread throughout the country. One of the new plaques

PHOTO COURTESY OF CLARENCE E. BISBEE, TWIN FALLS COUNTY HISTORICAL MUSEUM

This early Bisbee photo shows a bronze plaque commemorating the USS Maine and the 266 men killed in the 1898 explosion that destroyed it. The plaque was sculpted by Charles Keck and cast from bronze salvaged from the wreckage of the ship.

landed in Twin Falls in August that year and credit for bringing it to town was incorrectly given to U.S. Rep. Addison T. Smith. Addison Avenue is named for Smith, who was a Republican from Twin Falls.

But Smith quickly corrected the error with a letter to the editor of the *Twin Falls Times*. After a little research, the newspaper gave proper credit for the plaque to U.S. Sen. William Borah, a prominent Boise attorney.

The plaque is owned by the Twin Falls County Historical Society and displayed at the county museum.

Idaho's 3 Capitols and 2 Capitals

President Abraham Lincoln in 1863 signed a congressional act creating the territory of Idaho.

Idaho then encompassed the area that would become Montana and most of Wyoming. The population base — mostly gold miners chasing dreams of wealth — was then in the Clearwater region in what is now Idaho's panhandle. Lewiston became the territorial capital, and William H. Wallace, an old friend of Lincoln's, was appointed Idaho's first territorial governor.

PUBLIC DOMAIN
The first state capitol was built on State Street in Boise in the mid-1880s, when Idaho was still a territory. Construction began on the current capitol in 1905 and finished in 1920. This 1912 photograph shows the new capitol building under construction next to the old capitol (right). Central School is on the left. Both the school and the first capitol were razed after the completion of the new building.

Wallace was governor less than a year before being elected to Congress as a delegate from Washington State.

Lincoln appointed Caleb Lyon as the second governor in 1864. Lyon signed legislation to make Boise the capital soon after arriving in the territory, creating a bitter conflict between residents of northern Idaho and the burgeoning region of southern Idaho. Lewiston residents considered the move

illegal. Armed guards prevented Boise residents from moving the territorial seal and archives from Lewiston, and Lyon slipped quietly out of town.
The acting governor, Territorial Secretary Clinton Dewitt Smith, managed to move the seal and archives to Boise in 1865.
Meanwhile, the new territory proved too large to handle. In 1864, the Montana territory was carved out of the Idaho territory's northeast corner. And in 1866, Wyoming territory was created, leaving Idaho with its present-day boundaries.

Fugitive Evades the Hangman's Noose

Douglas Van Vlack was a man who liked to get his way.
And, he didn't like it when others presented barriers.
Van Vlack's young wife had recently divorced him. From that time on, Mildred Hook was doomed and she knew it, her family said later.
Van Vlack abducted Mildred at gunpoint and fled with her from their hometown of Tacoma, Wash., in November 1935.
Police picked up their trail in Boise. Idaho State trooper Fontaine Cooper and Henry Givens, a Twin Falls County sheriff's deputy, were on the lookout for the green 1931 Ford coupe on U.S. 30 near Buhl.
The *(Ellensburg, Wash.) Evening Daily Record* told the story of the fugitive's capture:
The officers tried to flag down Van Vlack when they spotted his car, but Van Vlack didn't stop.
Cooper and Givens caught up with Van Vlack just east of Buhl. They managed to get ahead of him and stopped his car.
Van Vlack shot Cooper as the state trooper attempted to pull him from the car. He shot Givens when the deputy tried to pull a gun on him.
Van Vlack sped away toward Filer.
Police soon after found Cooper dead and Givens dying, and a manhunt ensued.
About 8 a.m. the next morning, Van Vlack was found lying face down, exhausted, at the side of a road near Hollister.
Van Vlack told police that Mildred had hitchhiked home to Tacoma, but her battered body was found in a railroad culvert nearby. She had been shot in the head by her ex-husband.
Van Vlack later told Buhl Police Chief A.C. Parker that he had killed Mildred because her parents had called the police.
"If her folks had left us alone we would have been all right," Van Vlack told Parker. "She knew before she left Tacoma what was coming to her. I told her

father before I took her that if he didn't leave us alone, I'd kill her. That's why I did it."

Van Vlack had killed three people that night, but he was charged only with the murder of his ex-wife.

He was sentenced to be hanged at the Idaho State Prison, and in 1937, gallows were constructed inside an elevator shaft at the prison.

The day before his scheduled execution, Van Vlack's mother came to say goodbye.

As she left, Van Vlack jumped on a table, grabbed a catwalk and climbed to the top of the cell block.

"I'll be damned if I'll dangle on the end of a rope for the entertainment of a bunch of sightseers," he said.

Van Vlack jumped headfirst to his death on the prison floor.

When Blue Lakes Boulevard Met the Perrine Waterfall

Driving the boulevard in the early days was no easy task.

Early in the 20th century, Blue Lakes Boulevard began near the present-day Jerome County Airport, ran south through sagebrush to the top of the Snake River Canyon, followed an old Indian trail into the canyon and past the Blue Lakes, ferried the river, began the climb up the south wall of the canyon, ran under the falls at the Perrine Coulee and over the canyon rim, then shot straight south to Rock Creek.

"The scariest part of the trip was driving a team of horses under the Perrine Coulee," said Cleone Arrington, remembering the stories her mother used to tell.

Arrington's grandfather was a Mormon bishop who lived in Carey.

Occasionally, church business would require George Harris to travel to Albion. The trip from Carey to Albion took three days.

Arrington's mother, Florence, was a teenager when she would accompany her father on those trips.

Back then, that section of the boulevard — today known as Canyon Springs Road — ran under the waterfall, where irrigation water from the canal system dropped over the canyon's south rim on its way back to the Snake River.

When their wagon reached the waterfall, the skittish horses refused to go any farther, Arrington said.

George Harris would have to blindfold the horses and lead them on foot through the spray and the roar of the falling water. Florence Harris would drive the horses from the seat of the wagon.

PHOTO COURTESY CLARENCE E. BISBEE; RESTORED BY BLIP PRINTERS
This section of old Blue Lakes Boulevard — now Canyon Springs Road — ran behind the Perrine Coulee waterfall.

In later years, automobiles would replace horse-drawn wagons on the grade and under the waterfall, but the fear factor probably remained.

The road into the canyon — which was built by I.B. Perrine in the 1890s — was eventually rerouted to avoid the waterfall. The graveled road was finally widened and paved in the early 1970s.

Remnants of the old road can still be seen west of the coulee.

The Perrine Coulee — first a seasonal ditch — ran 12 months out of the year as a result of the creation of the canal system in 1905.

Blue Lakes Boulevard ended at the canyon once the rim-to-rim bridge was built in 1927.

HIDDEN HISTORY

A 'Merrie' Christmas from Twin Falls Photographers

The Christmas season has long been the most photographed time of the year. Here are a few holiday images captured by local photographers.

PHOTO COURTESY OF CLARENCE E. BISBEE, TWIN FALLS COUNTY HISTORICAL MUSEUM
'A Merrie Christmas' photo illustration created by Clarence E. Bisbee for his Christmas cards. Note the Twin Falls in the inset.

PHOTO COURTESY TWIN FALLS PUBLIC LIBRARY - DIGITAL COLLECTIONS
Twin Falls' first community Christmas tree at the City Park is seen in this early Clarence E. Bisbee photograph. Twin Falls High School can be seen across Shoshone Street from the park.

PHOTO COURTESY TWIN FALLS PUBLIC LIBRARY - DIGITAL COLLECTIONS
Main Avenue in Twin Falls is seen at Christmas 1957. The photo was taken by an unknown photographer at what is now Main Avenue and Gooding Street West, looking toward Shoshone Street. The Orpheum Theater, left, was showing the movie 'Time Limit,' starring Richard Widmark. The lighted Perrine Hotel sign can be seen on the right, along with others, including SavMor Drug Store, the Wray Cafe and the Top Hat Saloon.

Winter of 1948-49 Was Beautiful and Treacherous

Rex Reed still remembers the winter of 1948-49.

"It was beautiful — and treacherous," Reed said.

Reed had graduated from Filer High School the previous spring. He turned 18 and joined the National Guard during the worst winter to hit the Magic Valley since 1886.

His family lived at 4300 North and 2100 East — known then as Reed Road.

"The snow was bad at Christmas in '48, but the roads hadn't blown shut yet," Reed said.

After the New Year, temperatures dropped, making life miserable for many residents. The *Times-News* reported temperatures of 18 degrees below zero on Jan. 9, 1949, in Burley, Shoshone and Jerome.

Then the snow began to fall.

On Jan. 14, a paralyzing snowstorm hit the valley, followed by strong winds. Drifted snow clogged all area roads by the next morning, stranding hundreds of motorists and buses loaded with travelers.

Schoolhouses, gymnasiums, dance halls — public and private buildings alike — were used to house the stranded.

Reed said highway departments cleared what roads they could reach but left high walls of snow that quickly drifted shut behind the snowplows.

Many roads were abandoned when the snowplows no longer could pass through them, he said.

"Most of the north-south roads were blown shut, but U.S. 30 was closed a lot of the time," Reed said.

Many farmers in Reed's neighborhood had milk cows, but trucks couldn't get through to pick up milk.

"The cows had to be milked, but most guys were just dumping the milk on the ground," he said.

But not the Reed family.

The Reeds had a tall, horse-drawn hay wagon that had better ground clearance than most. Two horses could pull the wagon on dry ground, but four were needed to break through the snowdrifts.

Every day, the Reeds milked their cows, loaded 10-gallon cans of milk onto the hay wagon, then drove the horses through the snow to gather milk from a half-dozen neighbors.

The Reed hay wagon full of milk met the Sego milk truck at an intersection several miles away.

HIDDEN HISTORY

"Sego was good to us," Reed said. "They would take the full cans and drop off empties from the day before."

The snow and wind continued for a month.

"It got worse and worse, and the snow just kept piling up," he said.

That winter was the "worst in highway history," said memoirs by Art Hoult, the Idaho Highway Department maintenance supervisor for federal and state highways in eastern Idaho.

Continuous snow and high winds resulted in a blinding storm in early February 1949.

Snowplow drivers were marooned near American Falls, and caravans of travelers were stranded at Coldwater Camp near Raft River. Food and supplies were dropped to them by planes.

Many southern Idaho towns were cut off from the world as traffic came to a standstill.

Cattlemen reported animals by the hundreds frozen or starved to death. Trains were stalled on several occasions, including one that was stuck in snow west of

KELKER, O.A. (GUS), TIMES-NEWS
Horse-drawn wagons were used to haul feed to livestock when the snow clogged the roads. Bruce Robinson, and another man, both dressed in coats and cowboy hats, are seen standing on the back of the hay wagon in 1964. His son, Mike Robinson, holds the reins as his daughter, Holly Robinson, enjoys the ride.

Murtaugh.

Then the weather turned.

The *Times-News* warned on Feb. 16, 1949, that higher temperatures were coming, and residents should brace for flooding.

Snow melted quickly, but ice blocked the runoff's exit and houses flooded. "Water ran over the canal banks because the canal couldn't carry it all," Reed said.

A week later, headlines returned to the usual news.

"As far as the office of this county relief coordinator is concerned, the emergency caused by adverse weather conditions is over," declared DeWitt R. Young, Twin Falls County relief coordinator.

I.B. Perrine vs. the Beaver

Twenty years before he set out to irrigate what would become the Magic Valley, I.B. Perrine irrigated hundreds of acres in the Snake River Canyon.

In the 1880s, decades before the current canal system was formed, Perrine and his wife, Hortense, lived in the canyon on the north side of the river, in what was then Alturas County.

He also claimed land in the canyon south of the river, in what would soon become Twin Falls County.

Perrine developed an irrigated paradise with water that sprang from — and over — the canyon walls.

He planted thousands of fruit trees along the river where Blue Lakes Country Club and Canyon Springs Golf Course are now.

Perrine called his ranch "Blue Lakes" after the two crystal-clear blue lakes that feed Alpheus Creek, which runs through the country club today.

Perrine dug diversion ditches to direct spring water from the lakes to rows and rows of thirsty fruit trees and vineyards.

On the other side of the river, Perrine diverted seasonal runoff from the Perrine Coulee, a natural waterway that occasionally created a waterfall over an old Indian trail on the south canyon wall.

The Perrine Coulee now carries the tailings of the Twin Falls Canal Co.'s irrigation water that runs through the city of Twin Falls.

Perrine built up a lucrative business in the canyon, but not without incident.

A beaver surprised Perrine one evening, according to the *Twin Falls Weekly News*.

Perrine saw the beaver swimming in the lower lake, but was more intrigued by his guest than annoyed.

Then the beaver built a dam in Perrine's irrigation ditch, blocking the water from reaching the orchards.

Perrine admired the beaver's dam-building skill, he told the *Twin Falls Weekly* years later.

Every time Perrine tore down a dam, the beaver would rebuild it — bigger and better — by the next morning.

Then he realized the potential enormity of his problem. A perpetual water source plus thousands of trees could keep a beaver and an orchardman very busy undoing each other's work.

So, "much to his regret, (Perrine) loaded his shot gun with fine bird shot and laid in wait for the dam builder," wrote the Weekly.

Perrine peppered the beaver with shot, and it was never seen again.

Perrine went on to take the gold medal for fruit at the Paris World's Fair in 1900, and again at the Lewis and Clark Exposition in Portland, Ore., in 1905.

PHOTO COURTESY OF CLARENCE E. BISBEE, TWIN FALLS COUNTY HISTORICAL MUSEUM
I.B. Perrine settled in the Snake River Canyon in 1883. He called his home the 'Blue Lakes Ranch' for the two lakes that irrigated his orchards and vineyards.

PHOTO COURTESY OF CLARENCE E. BISBEE, TWIN FALLS COUNTY HISTORICAL MUSEUM
I.B. Perrine's Blue Lakes Ranch in the Snake River Canyon is seen in this early Clarence E. Bisbee photo.

Bisbee's Wife was his Muse

One of photographer Clarence E. Bisbee's favorite subjects was his wife, Jessie. Jessie M. Robinson and Bisbee met in Nebraska in 1904, but were separated two years later when Bisbee moved to Twin Falls to start his photography career.

Clarence first set up shop in a 16-by-28 tent on Main Avenue. He later moved his photography studio to a commercial building downtown.

All the while, he courted Jessie from afar, sending her photographs of the natural wonders that would be part of their life together if she would come to Idaho.
In June 1910, Clarence traveled to Nebraska to bring Jessie home to Twin Falls. They were married in Salt Lake City.
In 1914, the Bisbees hired architect E.H. Gates to build a home and studio at the corner of Second Avenue and Second Street East — now Hansen Street East.
The two planted a lush lawn and garden behind the studio.
Over the door of the studio were the words "Life and Art Are One."

PHOTOS COURTESY OF CLARENCE E. BISBEE, TWIN FALLS COUNTY HISTORICAL MUSEUM
Jessie and Clarence Bisbee took much pride in their home and photography studio in downtown Twin Falls. Jessie is seen lounging in their backyard and garden in these undated photographs.

The City of Rocks Stage Station

The journey from civilization to the Far West was shortened when the railroad came to Utah.
While many folks still were moving their belongings over the Oregon Trail, the railroad allowed easterners to visit the new frontier without taking a wagon train.
The closest train stop to southern Idaho was at Kelton, Utah, north of the Great Salt Lake.
The Kelton Road developed along Ben Holladay's 1864 mail route and became the preferred road between Kelton and Boise for stagecoaches and freight wagons.
From Kelton, the road ran north into Idaho, then turned west till it crossed the California Trail near the Twin Sisters at the southern edge of the City of Rocks.
The road then wound north through the City of Rocks in Cassia County and followed Birch Creek Canyon into what is now Oakley.

HIDDEN HISTORY

Holladay, known then as the Stagecoach King, established a stage line along the route and built three stage stops between Kelton and the Snake River in the mid-1860s.

The first station was built south of the City of Rocks. The second was the Rock Creek Station, south of present-day Hansen, and the third was the Desert Station, near where Rock Creek crosses U.S. 30 today.

William Trotter managed the City of Rocks stage station. His brother, Charles Trotter, managed the Rock Creek station.

The men had married two Walgamott sisters from Iowa, who cooked and kept clean beds for travelers.

PHOTO COURTESY OF CLARENCE E. BISBEE, TWIN FALLS COUNTY HISTORICAL MUSEUM
The Twin Sisters at the City of Rocks are seen in this early Clarence E. Bisbee photo. Ben Holladay, known as the Stagecoach King, built a home station near the Sisters in the mid-1860s.

Little remains of the stage station at the City of Rocks, said Kristen Bastis, parks service cultural resource ranger based in Almo. The stage stop was repurposed by homesteader John Moon in 1911, though.

Core samples taken from three or four logs in an old building at the Moon homestead have been dated to the stagecoach era, Bastis said.

William Trotter hired his wife's young brother, Charles Walgamott, to work at the City of Rocks stage stop. Walgamott later homesteaded at Shoshone Falls.

The third Walgamott sister, Lucy, married storekeeper Herman Stricker, and the couple ran the Stricker Store at the Rock Creek Stage Station.

PHOTO COURTESY OF CLARENCE E. BISBEE, TWIN FALLS COUNTY HISTORICAL MUSEUM
Charles S. Walgamott followed two of his sisters to Idaho, arriving in the Magic Valley in 1875. His sister Irene Trotter managed the Rock Creek Stage Stop with her husband, Charlie Trotter. His other sister married Bill Trotter, and the two ran the stage stop at the City of Rocks. Walgamott homesteaded at Shoshone Falls and introduced I.B. Perrine to the Blue Lakes in the Snake River Canyon.

Lind Automobile Co.: 1st Car Dealership in Twin Falls

Carl Lind built the first automobile dealership in town.
Lind Automobile Company sold Buick and Dodge Brothers' automobiles — and filtered gasoline at 25 cents per gallon.
In 1915, 618 cars were registered in Twin Falls County. By 1918, the number had grown to 3,520.

PHOTO COURTESY OF CLARENCE E. BISBEE, TWIN FALLS COUNTY HISTORICAL MUSEUM
Carl Lind stands in front of stacks of car tires at Lind Automobile Co. in Twin Falls. A gasoline pump can be seen on the right.

A Story of Family at Callen Corner

Rudolph Callen stood overlooking the landscape south of a new townsite in southern Idaho. The land was covered in sagebrush, but the location was good.
The following day in 1907, Callen filed on 55 acres on the corner of what would become Golf Course Road and 300 South near Jerome.

HIDDEN HISTORY

PHOTO COURTESY OF CLARENCE E. BISBEE, TWIN FALLS COUNTY HISTORICAL MUSEUM
Five of B.A. and Mary Callen's 10 sons fought in World War I. Seen from the left is Lester, Buenos, Richard, Ellsworth and Gus Callen. All five made it home alive.

After making his first payment and completing the paperwork to claim the land under the Carey Act, Callen returned to his young bride in Ontario, Ore. He planned to move to Idaho the following spring to begin work on his farm.

But Rudolph never made it back to Idaho. His wife, Mattie, died during childbirth, and Rudolph became ill and died in March 1908. Rudolph left his farm to his father, Buenos Ayres (B.A.) Callen.

B.A. Callen was born in 1860 in Arkansas. He and his wife Mary moved from Arkansas to Missouri, and then to Oregon in 1900.

When Rudolph died, B.A. and his son Buenos (pronounced byoo-nus) came to Idaho to claim Rudolph's farm. B.A.'s son Roscoe followed, and filed a claim on 55 acres near his father's farm. Mary and the rest of the family moved to Jerome in 1910. By then, Mary had given birth to 14 children, but three were gone.

When World War I broke out, five of the Callen boys — Lester, Buenos, Richard, Ellsworth and Gus — went off to fight. All five returned home alive. Tom, Christopher and Burt were too young to fight, said Tom's daughter, Jerome resident Blanche Peters.

Peters, 89, said all but one of her uncles settled near the original Callen homesite.

For extra income, the brothers cleared most of the land south of Jerome for their neighbors, and dragged the canals with a Fresno scraper to remove sediment.

Tom Callen bought the historic Shoe Sole, Point and Deep Creek ranches in Twin Falls County in the 1950s from the Utah Construction Co., Peters said. Her father then sold the Shoe Sole to his brother Richard.

"Uncle Dick ended up being a mail carrier," Peters said. "And Uncle Gus farmed north of Jerome, and served as the Jerome County Assessor."

Wilbur Hubbell: Buhl's National League Hero

Baseball pitcher Wilbur William Hubbell believed he had found the rainbow's end.

Hubbell was considered one of the best athletes in Idaho. Hubbell played on Buhl's 1914 Idaho State Champion high school football team, and excelled at baseball, basketball, track and swimming.

In 1919, the 22-year-old right-handed pitcher from Buhl jumped right to the majors. The 6-foot 2-inch hurler was touted as a coming star when he signed with the New York Giants.

But real success eluded him.

At the end of his rookie year, the Giants traded Hubbell to the Philadelphia Phillies.

In 1920, Hubbell won 9 of the 18 games that he pitched, and 9 of the 16 games he pitched in 1921.

In May 1922, the Phillies played the Brooklyn Dodgers in front of 2,500 fans at Shibe Park in Philadelphia.

In the opening inning, Hubble pitched to Tom Griffith, and Griffith drove a line drive, striking Hubble in the head.

"The ball flew like a projectile from a gun," wrote *The New York Times* that day.

The result was a severe concussion and a fractured skull. The fracture radiated in three directions above Hubbell's right ear, the paper reported.

"Hubbell is at the Stetson Hospital fighting for his life," the *Times* wrote. "The injury is probably fatal."

Phillies owner William Baker telegraphed Mrs. Hubbell in Buhl, telling her to come to Philadelphia immediately.

But Hubbell didn't die, and after recovering, he continued to play — albeit poorly — for the Phillies.

Several years later, he seemed to regain his confidence.

In 1924, the Times Herald of Cattaraugus, N.Y., wrote that Hubbell five years before, "had started in search of the end of the pitching rainbow. He made an exhaustive study of baseball, the Einstein theory, ragtime playing and Mah Jong in his efforts to locate the baseball pot of gold. But until the '24 season, his search seemed fruitless."

The season started well, but fizzled. The Phillies traded Hubbell to the Brooklyn Dodgers — the Brooklyn Robins, as the team was known then. In 1925, Hubble was traded to the minors.

HIDDEN HISTORY

He went on to play for the Minneapolis Millers, the Reading Keystones, the Seattle Indians, the Oakland Oaks, the Sacramento Senators, and finally, at the age of 35, the Portland Beavers in 1932.

Hubble died in Lakewood, Colo., in 1980, at the age of 83.

COURTESY PHOTO
Wilbur Hubbell of Buhl is seen at the age of 25 in this 1922 Philadelphia Phillies baseball card.

Fighting Alcohol Before the Prohibition

Attempts to keep alcohol out of the Magic Valley began years before the 18th Amendment.

Shortly after the village of Twin Falls was formed, Don Kingsley, who operated the ferry above Shoshone Falls, died in what was said to be an alcohol-related accident.

In April 1905, Kingsley tried to ferry an inebriated man — identified by the *Twin Falls Weekly News* only as M. Sullivan — across the Snake River. Kingsley somehow lost control of the boat and went over the falls. Sullivan survived by swimming ashore but was so drunk that he relayed three dissimilar stories to authorities.

Kingsley's body never was found but pieces of the boat and an oar were recovered below the falls.

Kingsley's apparent death stirred such controversy that the owner of the hotel in Shoshone Falls announced he would stop selling liquor.

Should the "proprietor do this, he will win the esteem of the decent element in Twin Falls who desire that the hotel should be in keeping with the magnificent attraction and a place to which nobody should be ashamed to go," the newspaper wrote the next month.

A local chapter of the Women's Christian Temperance Union was organized in 1906, just two years after the village of Twin Falls was formed. Decades before, the national WCTU was formed to create a "sober and pure world," according to its publications.

The local citizenry was split. Some wanted to abolish alcohol under a local-option prohibition law. Others disagreed, said historian Jim Gentry.

The Twin Falls County Taxpayers' League tried to stop the momentum for prohibition, citing the loss of needed revenues from liquor licenses, Gentry

wrote in his book, "In the Middle and on the Edge."
Businessmen and ministers then jumped into the fight.
One business came up with the slogan, "Don't drink intoxicating liquor. But if you must drink, drink the best at the Hotel Perrine Bar."
In November 1909, Twin Falls County voted to abolish liquor, and saloons in the county closed by February 1910. In 1916, the entire state of Idaho went "dry," Gentry said.
The 18th Amendment to the Constitution was ratified in January 1919 and took effect the following year.
It was repealed by the 21st Amendment in 1933.

PHOTO COURTESY OF CLARENCE E. BISBEE, TWIN FALLS COUNTY HISTORICAL MUSEUM
The Twin Falls chapter of the Women's Christian Temperance Union is seen destroying illegal drinks along Shoshone Street North in this 1922 Bisbee photograph.

Air Force Jet, Car Collision on U.S. 93

Mrs. Clarence Smith knew the airplane was in trouble when she saw it, so she kept her eyes on its lights until it passed overhead.
That night in 1955, the Smith family was on its way from their home in Twin

HIDDEN HISTORY

PHOTO COURTESY OF CLARENCE E. BISBEE, TWIN FALLS COUNTY HISTORICAL MUSEUM
U.S. Air Force Lieut. Clyde Seller was flying a T33 air force jet to Mountain Home when mechanical problems forced him to land the jet on Hwy 93 in December 1955. Seller tried to leapfrog a Chevrolet station wagon during the landing, sending both vehicles into a spin

Falls to a Christmas party in Jerome. As they crossed the Perrine Memorial Bridge in their Chevrolet station wagon, they spotted the lights of a plane coming at them, barely 500 feet off the ground.

Above them, U.S. Air Force Lt. Clyde Seller was preparing to make an emergency landing on U.S. 93.

Seller was flying a T33 Air Force jet from Williams Air Force Base in Arizona to Mountain Home when his instruments failed at 40,000 feet. Unable to see lights at the Twin Falls Municipal Airport, Seller looked for another place to land.

He circled his jet three times over Highway 93 north of Twin Falls before deciding to bring it down on the highway. The Smith family spotted the plane southbound on its third pass.

Seller turned and made a northbound landing on the two-lane highway north of the bridge. According to news reports, Seller flew the jet under high-powered electric lines before touching the ground.

The 100-mph landing would have been perfect, if it hadn't been for the 40-mph

station wagon in the road.
Mrs. Smith knew almost immediately what had hit them.
"There was a flash of light, an explosion like a bomb," Mrs. Smith told the *Times-News* after the wreck. "The car rocked violently but while things made by man were demolished, things made by God remained intact."
Sellers tried to brake the plane. Smith — unaware of the aircraft behind him — wasn't in a big hurry.
When a crash was imminent, Seller tried to get airborne again, but he clipped the top of the car with a wing as he took off. The car lost its roof and rear left door, and the plane lost a wing tank.
No one in the wreck suffered serious injuries.
The photos that accompany this story were taken by KLIX-TV (Channel 11) film director Vic Graybeal a few months after the station went on the air.
The new television station — a sister station to KLIX radio — was the first in Twin Falls. The KLIX stations were split in 1957, when Utah businessman Abe Glasmann bought the pair, then sold off the radio station. The television station then became KMVT — for Magic Valley Television.

Before the Cottage Motel Fell Apart

Tucked away between Barry Rental and Valley House are 10 tiny rental homes that have seen better days — so much, in fact, their days may be numbered.
Many decades ago, George Ryan bought little houses in Twin Falls and moved them amid a grove of shade trees along Addison Avenue West.
Ryan turned the row of buildings into a campground of cottages to accommodate tourists traveling U.S. 30.
Ryan made his home in a house that he moved from the St. Edwards School in Twin Falls. He converted another house into a small store — complete with a nickel slot machine — to serve the clientele of the Ryan Motel.
One cottage was a granary that he converted into a kitchenette.
"He bought every tiny little thing that he could move in," said Evelyn LeClair.
Most of the houses have no foundations but sit on cinder blocks.
Evelyn and her husband, Lloyd, and Lloyd's parents, Joe and Anna LeClair, purchased the motel in 1956.
Two years later, a bar customer backed across Addison and knocked over the Ryan Motel sign. The LeClairs changed the business' name to the Cottage Motel when they replaced the sign, Evelyn said.
Joe and Anna lived in a rental house across town at Main Street and Blue Lakes Boulevard. The two cared for their elderly landlord, who lived in a small house

HIDDEN HISTORY

next door. When the landlord died, the LeClairs inherited both houses and moved them to the Cottage Motel.

The LeClairs ran the business for 33 years, and business was good for the first 15.

"That was before the Interstate and motorhomes," Evelyn said. "Running a motel is like owning a dairy. You've got to be there in the morning. You've got to be there at night. And in between, you do the laundry."

By 1989, the LeClairs were ready to get out of the motel business, said Michael Leclair, Evelyn's son. Michael's family sold the motel for $90,000 to a California couple who just happened to stay there while traveling through Idaho.

Two years later, the couple sold the motel — for $200,000 — to Jerome businessman Jim Jurgens, said Michael.

Jurgens rented out the cottages by the month until his death in May.

The cottages have fallen into disrepair and residents are moving out. The future of the cottages is now uncertain.

ASHLEY SMITH, TIMES-NEWS
People were evicted from their homes at 485 Addison Ave. W. because of poor living conditions, electrical problems and natural gas leaks.

Tom Blodgett: Minister with a Controversial Side

Tom Blodgett came to town more dead than alive.

The retired minister drove 40 bootleggers out of business in Wichita, Kan., and started the national Men's Gospel Team movement before becoming seriously ill.

Blodgett came to Hansen to restore his health, but ended up rejuvenating the town.

In the early 1920s, Blodgett turned the "dozing hamlet" of Hansen into a "vital, throbbing community," said a November 1924 article in *Sunset Magazine*.

Hansen had one church building — owned by the Methodist Episcopal Church — when Blodgett arrived in 1921. A minister from out of town held Sunday morning services for a congregation of a dozen souls.

The town of 200 residents "tolerated the church instead of supporting it," said the *Sunset* article. Donations were paid to church members "in order to be rid of them." The Ladies' Aid Society provided the church's only activities, and "men (in church) were as scarce as hens' teeth."

Blodgett was assigned as minister of the Hansen church in 1923. He grew the congregation from a handful to more than 100 in the first year. Donations to the church increased from $500 per year to $2,500 in 1924.

Decades later, Hansen resident Lena Bohrn told the *Times-News* that Blodgett "had people wrapped around his finger."

A town mired in apathy was lifted out of the muck, figuratively and literally, by the new preacher, said the *Sunset* article.

A mountain of basement dirt was left standing on the new school grounds because town officials were reluctant to spend money to remove it. On his second Sunday at the pulpit, Blodgett solicited the help of 25 men with 50 horses to level the piled dirt into a playground ready for seeding.

Next, Blodgett gathered the town's 15 businessmen and formed the Hansen Business Men's Association. A few week's later, the group sponsored a successful "Corn Show Day." A three-day farmers' institute soon followed, raising much-needed civic pride.

Blodgett was designated director of the "Community Program." The scope of the program reached into all facets of life in Hansen — education, recreation, public health, finance and roads.

In 1924, Blodgett began promoting mining stock from the pulpit. He sold stock in a calcite mine in Wyoming that was later described by duped investors as a fly-by-night scheme. Many folks in town bought into the so-called scheme, and lost a considerable amount of money.

Blodgett then moved to Twin Falls where he owned and operated the *Idaho Citizen* newspaper. He died of cancer about a year later.

But some in town never lost faith in Blodgett, despite their losses, wrote Hansen historian Francis Harris.

Hansen townsfolk "either hated or loved him," Harris said.

"But for a few years he infused the community with a vision of what residents of a small rural town can accomplish."

The Great Dinosaur Caper of 1963

In honor of what some in town have called "the greatest senior stunt ever," the Twin Falls High School rock was recently painted and adorned with plastic

HIDDEN HISTORY

dinosaurs by the class of 1963.

Fifty years ago, members of the senior class travelled to Gooding County and absconded with a large green dinosaur from the Rimview Cafe in Bliss. Somehow the kids managed to return to Twin Falls with the 25-foot-long stegosaurus named Dinney and placed it on the rooftop of the high school. Back then, there was no freeway through southern Idaho. Families travelling U.S. 30 on their way to Boise stopped at the 24-hour Rimview to grab a bite to eat and fill up at the gas station next door.

In front of the cafe was a parking lot and on the other side of the parking lot was "Dinneyland," where the fiberglass dinosaur roamed. Actually, Dinney's feet were embedded in concrete, but that didn't deter the students.

State patrolman Walter Kirtly, who lived in Bliss, heard rumors that something might happen to the dinosaur. But sometime during the night of May 20, 1963, the stegosaurus disappeared from right under his nose.

That night, a long parade of cars and pickups headed out of Twin Falls. Later, several dozen high school seniors descended on the little cafe and gas station in Bliss.

Most of the students were there as a diversion, said John Kelker, son of then-*Times-News* editor Gus Kelker.

John Kelker wrote in his 50-year reunion memoirs that he and his friends parked in front of Dinneyland to block the view from the restaurant. The students created a ruckus inside the restaurant and at the gas pumps, while other students sawed the dinosaur from its perch.

Dinney was loaded onto a truck, covered with a tarp, and hauled to Twin Falls, where it was found atop the high school gymnasium roof the next morning. A large number "63" was taped to the dinosaur's side.

A lot of planning went into the caper, said Jerry Kuykendall, 1963 senior class president. But there was some luck involved too.

A Buhl cop stopped the convoy of cars as students drove through town with a dinosaur's tail hanging out from under a tarp at 2 a.m. But the cop didn't bother to look under the tarp, Kuykendall said.

Kuykendall's classmates didn't let him participate in the caper — they knew they would later need him as a mediator for the group.

Steve Woodall, TFHS class of 1964, remembers the stunt.

"Initially, everybody was pretty proud of themselves for pulling it off," Woodall said. "However, when talk of a lawsuit and possible criminal charges were brought up, attitudes changed in a hurry."

Soon, word was out that other schools were planning to steal it off Twin Falls' roof, and Dinney was moved to a temporary home in a local barn.

MYCHEL MATTHEWS

Dr. Edward Stewart Robinson owned the cafe, Dinney and Dinneyland, as well as Shoshone Ice Caves in Lincoln County. Robinson told the Twin Falls weekly "*Star*" that it was the third attempt to steal the dinosaur in five years, and he was tired of the pranks. Robinson promised to sue the students, the school, and Principal George Staudaher for "interruption of business."

The dinosaur caper was reported on national television, and even Paul Harvey told the story on his national radio broadcast. According to Kuykendall, *Life* magazine changed its plans to feature the story when Robinson threatened to file charges against the guilty parties.

"The magazine didn't want to give him any free publicity after he was being such a jerk about it," Kuykendall said Wednesday.

The students were prepared to pay to repair the damages to the dinosaur, but Robinson wanted more money. In the end, the town paid $1,500 to $2,000 to keep Robinson from filing charges.

"The amazing thing is how it brought the community together," said Kuykendall. "The whole town made sure we had enough money to pay off Robinson."

Twin Falls County Sheriff Jim Benham "even took the Gooding sheriff on a wild goose chase 'looking' for the dinosaur," Kuykendall said. "Benham knew where the dinosaur was hid all along."

Dinney eventually returned home with the help of high school students and parents, probably on the same truck that was used to steal him, Kuykendall said.

Robinson later moved the dinosaur to Shoshone Ice Caves, where he still stands. (Dinney is not the largest dinosaur — the one with the caveman sitting on his neck — at the ice caves, Kuykendall said.)

John Anderson, 1963 TFHS graduate and unofficial spokesman for the "Great Dinosaur Caper," said he is sure the statute of limitations has run out on this case. He also said that no dinosaurs were harmed or killed during the escapade.

MYCHEL MATTHEWS, TIMES-NEWS
The Twin Falls High School rock is seen after being decorated by the Class of 1963 for its 50-year reunion.

HIDDEN HISTORY

Some Dreams are too Big

Success can be intoxicating — and intoxication can cause irrational thinking. So, drunk on success, Magic Valley pioneers made some grandiose and somewhat questionable plans to expand agriculture's reach.

The Twin Falls Irrigation Tract, including the north- and south-side tracts, irrigated about a half-million acres of fertile crop land with water from the Snake River at Milner Dam. When complete, the project was the largest and most successful Carey Act reclamation project in the nation.

In the late 1910s, developers made plans to more than double the farmable acres in the valley and bring another 75,000 homesteaders to Twin Falls and Owyhee counties.

PHOTO COURTESY OF CLARENCE E. BISBEE; RESTORED BY BLIP PRINTERS
The Milner Dam and Riverside Inn are seen in this Clarence E. Bisbee photo. The Great Brudeau Project aimed to take water from the dam to 600,000 acres of desert.

It was called the "Great Bruneau Project."

The plan was to build a canal — even bigger than the south-side canal — to take water from Milner Dam to 600,000 acres of desert west of Buhl. The canal was to run parallel to the high-line canal south of the Snake River. If complete, the Bruneau project would have made the south-side canal system 140 miles long.

The Bruneau tract would have begun near Balanced Rock west of Castleford, then fanned north and west to Bruneau Sand Dunes southwest of Mountain Home.

The project would have brought a huge economic boon to the town of Buhl. Promoters estimated the project would create 10,000 construction jobs lasting three years.

But the project had its obstacles: A post-World War I agricultural depression left farmers heavily in debt. A severe drought in 1919 gave farmers and investors cause to worry about water supplies.

And by 1921, most of the original developers of the Twin Falls tract were gone. Walter Filer had moved out of state. Peter Kimberly, Stanley Milner and Frank Buhl were all dead. Only I.B. Perrine remained.

The Great Bruneau Project never got off the drawing board.

The KKK in the Magic Valley

For 50 years after the federal government told it to disband, the local Ku Klux Klan laid low — until its resurgence in the 1920s, when the Klan came to town to recruit members.

By 1922, the KKK had become a minor political power in the West, with a focus on white Protestant dominance over blacks, Catholics and Jews. The movement got a foothold in California, then spread to Oregon and Washington.

The Klan pushed to increase its membership that year, claiming 35,000 members in Oregon alone, wrote Eckard V. Toy in "The Invisible Empire in the West: Toward a New Historical Appraisal of the Ku Klux Klan of the 1920s."

In January 1923, the Rev. Lew Burger, a KKK leader and motivational speaker from New York, spoke at the IOOF Hall in Buhl.

The *Buhl Herald* praised Burger's speaking style and said a dozen hooded Klansmen handed out membership forms at two of his lectures. Klan dues were $3.50 a year, plus a $10 joining fee. The newspaper did not report whether a Buhl branch — or klavern — was formed.

The next month, Burger spoke to a group in Idaho Falls and claimed that 38 members of Congress were Klan members.

Curiously, H.W. Evans, imperial wizard of the Klan, declared that he had never heard of Burger and that no member of the Klan was allowed to discuss Klan membership, says a Feb. 15, 1923, Associated Press news article.

Later that year, the KKK came close to taking control of the Twin Falls city

HIDDEN HISTORY

election; Klan candidates were narrowly defeated.

In 1924, about 150 men and women in full Klan regalia held a day-long rally at the Twin Falls County Fairgrounds.

A year later, Buhl's only black resident received a threat from the Klan. Henry Field had run a shoeshine parlor in town since 1915.

Field discussed the state of local banks after the post-World War I agricultural depression. Apparently, the Klan didn't approve of the discussion and threatened him in a letter. Although others had joined in the conversation, Field was the only one threatened.

PUBLIC DOMAIN
Ku Klux Klan parade through counties in Northern Virginia bordering on the District of Columbia, 1922.

The Turf Club Has Been Here and There

DATELINE: TWIN FALLS (Or was it Hansen?)

The Turf Club on Falls Avenue was not always within the city limits of Twin Falls.

But Hansen?

Sort of.

In the late 1940s, Alcoholics Anonymous took an active role against selling liquor by the drink, and some towns in Idaho listened.

The city of Twin Falls rejected attempts to pass liquor-by-the-drink laws in 1947 and 1952. But bars in Hansen could sell alcohol by the drink.

In those days, the Turf Club sat a mile outside the northern limits of Twin Falls, but apparently the owners felt threatened by its possible annexation into a town that would outlaw its business.

So somehow, Hansen, a town nearly 10 miles southeast of the Turf Club, annexed a strip of land along Falls Avenue — the club included — in July 1953, according to local historian Jim Gentry.

"The owners probably talked the town into it," Gentry said. "The Turf Club certainly had more to gain by it than the town did."

Hansen repealed the annexation the following month, after the town was hit with a slew of lawsuits.

Tom Callen, O.A. Rambo and Bob Wildman started the business in 1946, said Steve Soran, a co-owner of the Turf Club today.

"The Inkspots were the opening act," said Soran, whose family has owned the Turf Club since the late 1960s.

"It was a fancy little gig," he said. "The place had 14 slot machines, gaming tables and the banquet room."

Its signature neon martini-glass sign was installed sometime between 1952 and 1954, Soran said.

The Turf Club got its name from a racetrack across the street. Local cattlemen raced their horses at the track where Frontier Field is now, he said.

MYCHEL MATTHEWS, TIMES-NEWS
The Turf Club's signature sign is photographed in 2013. The neon sign, installed in the early 1950s, recently grabbed the attention of the National Trust for Historic Preservation.

Making Hay when the Sun Shines

Remnants of old wooden haystackers still scatter the Magic Valley landscape. But many people today wouldn't know one if they saw it in a field.

These three pictures taken by unidentified photographers around 1915 show hay harvest in full swing.

The most labor-intensive method was to hand pitch the loose hay to the top of the stack. Men would carry pitchforks full of hay to the top, climbing the stack as it grew.

Other methods included wooden stacking implements powered by horses or oxen.

An overshot hay stacker — sometimes called a jayhawk — held a 600-pound load of hay on a "sweep bucket" that would lift and dump the hay onto the stack. The most common method used locally was the gin pole stacker — which resembled a partially disassembled teepee — that would lift, swing and lower a load of hay into place on the stack.

It is said that hay can grow in any part of the country where weeds will grow.

PHOTO COURTESY OF CLARENCE E. BISBEE, TWIN FALLS COUNTY HISTORICAL MUSEUM
An overshot hay stacker — sometimes called a jayhawk — held a load of hay on a "sweep bucket" that would lift and dump the hay onto the stack.

PHOTO COURTESY OF CLARENCE E. BISBEE, TWIN FALLS COUNTY HISTORICAL MUSEUM
Stacking hay by pitchfork was hard work.

PHOTO COURTESY OF CLARENCE E. BISBEE, TWIN FALLS COUNTY HISTORICAL MUSEUM
Stacking hay using gin poles was easier than by pitchfork. Oxen or horses provided the power.

Vegas Vic Continues to Wave in Twin Falls

Even if you've never been to Las Vegas, you may have seen Vegas Vic. Or maybe it was Wendover Will. For years, Vegas Vic has towered over Fremont Street in Sin City, waving at gamblers and pointing to the Pioneer Club below.
For almost as long, Wendover Will has performed a nearly identical job in West Wendover, Nev., directing folks to the Stateline Casino.
Much larger than life, both neon icons have become symbols of their towns. And along U.S. 93, south of Twin Falls, Idaho's own version of Vic — or Will — waved at tourists bound for Nevada.

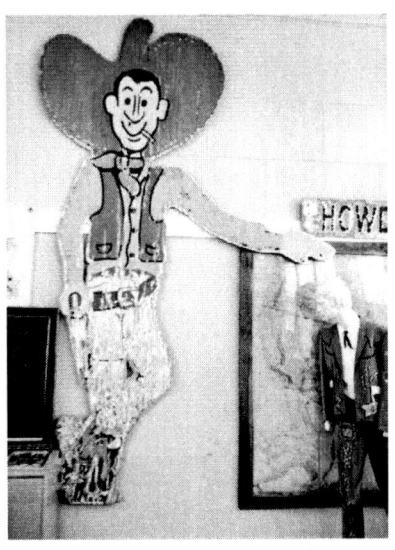

MYCHEL MATTHEWS, TIMES-NEWS
This cowboy stood alongside a billboard on U.S. 93 south of Twin Falls, advertising a Nevada casino in the 1950s and '60s. It now greets visitors at the Twin Falls County Museum.

The 10-foot-tall, flat cowboy stood next to a roadside billboard advertising one of the casinos during the 1950s and '60s. Some remember the cowboy waving from Ken Roundy's Deluxe Motor Lodge on Main Avenue West in Twin Falls.
Now he stands inside the Twin Falls County Historical Museum, a little weather-beaten and faded. He even sports a bullet hole above his lip, an injury he sustained during his roadside vigil.
But the question remains: Which casino does the flat cowboy represent? Is he Vegas Vic or Wendover Will?
The cowboy's image first appeared in 1947, commissioned by the Las Vegas Chamber of Commerce. In 1951, owners of the Pioneer Club turned the image into a giant neon sign, complete with a waving arm, bobbing cigarette, and a recording that boomed "Howdy Pardner!" every 15 minutes.
A similar image reappeared the following year in Wendover at the Stateline Casino, with the addition of a six-gun on his hip.
Twin Falls flat cowboy has a six-gun and a "Howdy Pardner" greeting. Wendover Will and Vegas Vic still stand.
Vic stopped waving in 1966 when actor Lee Marvin and his film crew stayed in the Mint Hotel across the street. Legend has it that one of the filmmakers shot

HIDDEN HISTORY

Vic to silence the "Howdy Pardner" greeting that kept him awake. Later, a Las Vegas minister married Vic and the nearby neon sign "Sassy Sally" when the Fremont Street Experience was constructed in the 1990s. The Pioneer Club closed soon after and is now a souvenir shop.

Will, the taller of the two cowboys, was included in the city seal when West Wendover was incorporated in 1991. He was moved away from the casino and now welcomes traffic into town. Will is cited in the Guinness Book of Records as the World's Largest Mechanical Cowboy.

PHOTO COURTESY OF MARK HUFSTETLER
Wendover Will stands in downtown West Wendover, Nev., welcoming visitors to town. The sign used to stand at the Stateline Casino.

A New Search for an Old School Pool

There is something addictive about reading old newspapers. Just ask Steve Woodall.

Woodall is the self-proclaimed historian of the Facebook group, "You Might Be from Twin Falls, Idaho ..." and he's been digging through decades of digital newspapers trying to debunk historical rumors.

One mystery he recently solved is whether Twin Falls' first high school ever had a swimming pool.

The answer is no, but it is easy to see how such a rumor started, Woodall said. Twin Falls High School opened in February 1912, on Shoshone Street next to the Twin Falls County Courthouse. It was hailed as the best equipped high school in the Northwest.

The building, which was torn down in 1980, morphed over a 70-year period from a high school, to a combination senior/junior high school, then finally to a junior high.

"After seeing all of the confusion on the issue that existed at the time, I can fully understand why the confusion continues today," Woodall wrote in a recent post on the group's Facebook page.

As the young town grew, the school district planned to add wings to the building for seventh and eighth grades.

The 1919 expansion plan included a swimming pool partly because Buhl had a municipal pool, but Twin Falls did not, Woodall said.

Records show that a pool was dug at the high school after private money was promised for the project. The pool, however, was never completed and new wings were built on Washington School, at the northeast end of Shoshone Street, instead.

But the idea of a pool in the school still persists.

Some believe the school's "little gym" was once a pool — due to the odd placement of windows in the room. The pool, some say, was replaced by the gym and an auditorium was built over it.

But Woodall, who lives in Boise, has moved on to debunk another rumor.

"Thanks, Steve," wrote fellow Facebooker Jim Langley. "A job well done! Your next assignment: Did Mr. Waite, the Washington School janitor, really wear his suspenders to bed?"

A Grand View

PHOTOS COURTESY OF CLARENCE E. BISBEE, TWIN FALLS COUNTY HISTORICAL MUSEUM
C.E. Bisbee climbed to the top of a water tower to capture this image. Main Avenue is seen on the right. The Perrine Hotel is seen at the west corner of Main Avenue and Shoshone Street.

A photographer needed a high vantage point to fit an entire town into his camera's view finder.

A water tower between Second Street and Main Avenue South provided just the right perch in early Twin Falls. The tower was located near where Krengle's Hardware stands today.

Clarence E. Bisbee climbed this tower as it was being built and got a view of the town from the top.

HIDDEN HISTORY

The street on the right is Main Avenue. The Perrine Hotel is seen at the west corner of Main and Shoshone Street.
The street on the left is Second Street South. An alley runs down the center of the photo.
The Jerome Butte is visible in the distance.
Water was hauled to the tower from nearby Rock Creek.

The Most American Thing in America

When early Idahoans found themselves isolated from culture, entertainment and education, the Chautauqua — a sort of traveling circus for adult education — provided the fix.
The circuit developed from the Chautauqua Institution — a summer educational camp in New York — in the late 19th century. The movement spread across the country, bringing theater, opera, musicians and lectures to newly settled towns such as Twin Falls.
The Chautauqua (pronounced shuh-TAW-kwaw) has been called "a carnival for thinking people." President Theodore Roosevelt called it "the most American thing in America."
Three-time presidential candidate Williams Jennings Bryan — who made various trips to Twin Falls after the turn of the 20th century — was the most popular speaker to travel the circuit but never spoke at a Chautauqua in Twin Falls.
The Chautauquas were held in large tents and lasted several days at each location. Entertainers or lecturers rotated shifts through the circuit.
In 1925, Gilbert and Sullivan's "The Mikado" began March 26 in Abbeville, La., and finished Sept. 6 in Sidney, Mont., stopping in Preston, Pocatello, Twin Falls, Gooding, Boise, Nampa and Parma toward the end of the tour.
In their heyday during the mid-1920s, Chautauquas appeared in thousands of towns across the nation. By the 1940s, other forms of entertainment, such as radio and motion pictures, had replaced the circuit.

Your Guess is as Good as Mine

It has been said that a picture is worth a thousand words.
Unfortunately, pictures are mute. When they have no inscriptions, all we can do is marvel at the details in the photo as we allow our thoughts to drift off into someone else's lifetime.
Take, for example, an undated photograph of homesteaders in Twin Falls

County. While their prove-up shack seems to be lacking the ordinary comforts of home, it is obvious that the family came from a more prosperous past. A fancy parlor table stands at the far left. A bird cage — complete with resident — hangs from the front eave of the shack. A wooden rocking chair sits at the front door, and a state-of-the-art buggy stands in contrast to the ramshackle barn in the background.

The photo was taken on a good day; everyone is eating watermelon. And as for the portrait of the cowboy and his horse, your guess is as good as mine.

PHOTOS COURTESY OF CLARENCE E. BISBEE, TWIN FALLS COUNTY HISTORICAL MUSEUM

Shoshone Falls: An Unfulfilled Memorial

Before potatoes — and Evel Knievel — the Niagara of the West was this valley's claim to fame.

"It is hard to imagine anything in nature more picturesque or sublime," visitor Charles Nelson Teeter wrote in 1865.

In 1900, proponents tried to have Shoshone Falls designated as a national park. Congress opposed the move, but the falls captured the nation's attention. That October, the *Chicago Tribune* devoted a full page to photos of Shoshone Falls, Twin Falls and Blue Lakes.

The scenic view of the falls begged for more recognition. At the end of World War I, a memorial park, dedicated to returning war heroes, was proposed for the falls on the south side of the Snake River Canyon. The Shoshone Falls Memorial Park Association was organized in 1919.

That summer, the association's board hired young California landscape architect Florence Yoch to draft a plan for an elaborate park, complete with trees, benches and resting areas.

Yoch blazed a trail through a male-dominated profession and became nationally known for her architectural designs. She later designed the David O. Selznick estate in Beverly Hills, the Getty House gardens in Los Angeles, and various landscapes for film sets, including Tara in "Gone with the Wind." The canyon land south of the Snake River, however, was owned by various entities — private and public — making the park plan nearly impossible to implement. The Twin Falls County commissioners proposed a memorial bridge to span the Snake River Canyon at Shoshone Falls as an alternative to the park.

Neither project got past the drawing board at the time, but the land eventually was donated to the city of Twin Falls and developed into today's park.

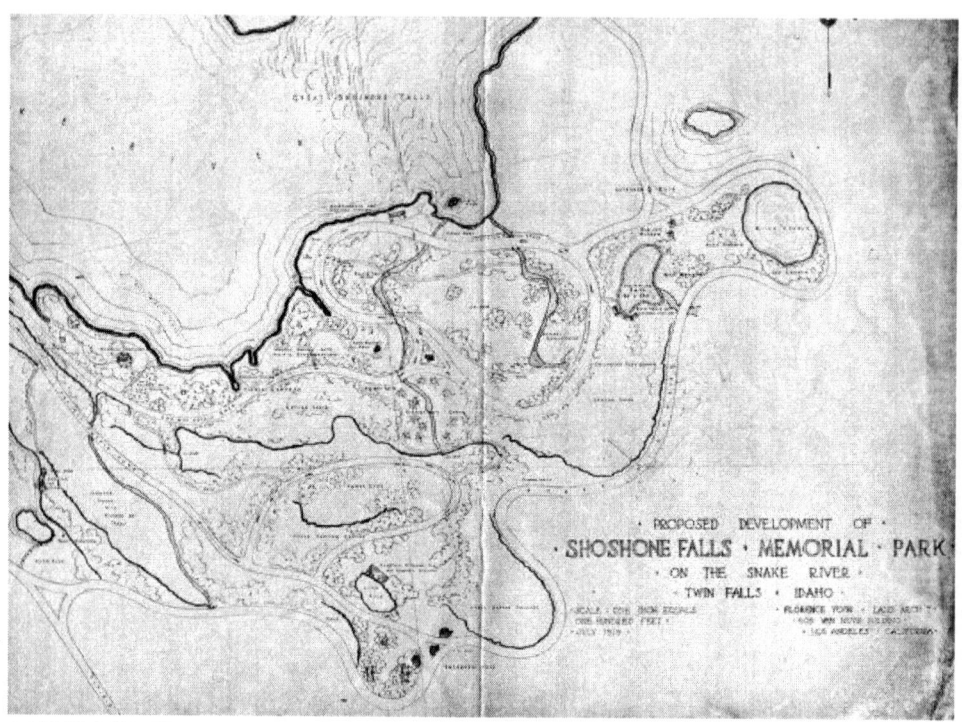

PHOTO COURTESY OF TWIN FALLS PARKS AND RECREATION DEPARTMENT
This segment of a drawing shows the short-lived plan to crete a memorial park at Shoshone Falls, designed by California landscape architect Florence Yoch in 1919.

Long Defunct Towns in Twin Falls County

Don't blink or you'll miss it.

About three miles west of Twin Falls, railroad tracks cross U.S. 30. Today, this intersection is known as "Curry Crossing" — but years ago the town of Curry flourished there.

Nearly all that remains of the original town is the old Union School building – which now houses the Twin Falls County Historical Museum – built in 1914.

MYCHEL MATTHEWS

Curry is not alone in its hidden history. There are far more defunct towns in Twin Falls County than incorporated municipalities.

One of the oldest towns in the county was Rock Creek, located seven miles south of Hansen. Rock Creek had a post office by 1871 and a school by 1879. The town sat near the junction of the Old Oregon Trail and the Kelton Road, southeast of Stricker Ranch.

Artesian City was a town that straddled the Twin Falls and Cassia county line, south of Murtaugh Lake. It was homesteaded in the 1870s and became a town in 1909, two years after Twin Falls County was created. The town was named for the area's artesian water.

The area near Milner Dam, in eastern Twin Falls County, was first called "the Cedars" by emigrants on the Oregon Trail. The Cedars was their last stop on the Snake River until they reached Kanaka Rapids north of modern-day Buhl. The boom town of Milner began with the construction of the Milner Dam, which was completed in 1905. At one time, nearly 2,000 people lived at Milner, including 1,500 construction workers. The town boasted two hotels, a bank, stores and a school. Milner was named for Stanley B. Milner, president of the Twin Falls Land and Water Co.

The town of Bickel, which sat a few miles northwest of Murtaugh, was named for Paul S. Bickel, chief engineer of the Twin Falls irrigation project.

Several towns in southwestern Twin Falls County have disappeared over the years. Amsterdam, north of Hollister, was settled around 1910 by Dutch immigrants from Iowa. Berger was an agricultural center on Desert Creek, settled in 1908. Farther west still, Roseworth was settled as a homestead in 1884 and had a post office by 1896.

Other towns in the county that have dried up over the years include Abby, Cephas, Alta, Butte, Clear Lakes, Austin, Haggardt and Peavey.

PHOTO COURTESY OF TWIN FALLS COUNTY HISTORICAL MUSEUM
In this photo by an unknown photographer, townsfolk are seen in 1904 at teh Perrine and Burton General Merchandise building on a main street of Milner.

HIDDEN HISTORY

Bisbee's Sense of Humor Showed a Soft Spot for Bunnies

Photographer Clarence E. Bisbee was serious about his work — most of the time.

Bisbee photographed hundreds of portraits, street scenes and landscapes for posterity; he and his wife Jessie photographed animals for fun.

The Bisbees kept a passel of tame bunnies at their home in Twin Falls. They kept even more on their land in the Snake River Canyon. The photos of their pets reveal a whole different side of the man and his art.

One photo shows bunnies Sunlight and Silver conversing on an early "candlestick" telephone. Another shows Silver driving a rooster-drawn wagon full of eggs. The third photo is a portrait of Blossom, Daffodil, Hope and Sage in front of the Bisbees' hearth.

PHOTOS COURTESY OF CLARENCE E. BISBEE, TWIN FALLS COUNTY HISTORICAL MUSEUM
Jessie and Clarence Bisbee staged many photos using their pet bunnies: Sunlight, Silver, Blossom, Daffodil, and Hope.

There's Magic in this Valley

This arid region of Idaho was labeled "Sage Brush Plains" on many 19th century maps. Later, irrigation water was added, and – poof – the desert became rich farm land, as if by magic.

Of course, it wasn't quite that easy. But the idea of such a magical reclamation of the land made an effective marketing tool for local promoters.

The city of Twin Falls — the commercial center of this irrigated region — was soon known as the "Magic City." That is, until another town in Idaho objected.

Apparently, the city of Caldwell had claimed the title of Magic City long before Twin Falls was founded.

But the name stuck in the minds of folks in town. Many businesses – like

Magic City Feed and Fuel Co. in Twin Falls — continued to use the term in their names.

As surrounding towns began to prosper, the area described as "magic" began to grow. By 1929, the *Twin Falls Daily News* had used the term "Magic Valley" when referring to the greater Twin Falls area.

In September 1937, newspaper publisher R.S. Tofflemire — of both the *Daily News* and the *Idaho Evening Times* — gathered his department heads specifically to coin a catchy nickname for the entire region.

Sun Valley was gaining fame nationally, so south-central Idaho needed a name that would be good for tourism and present a positive image of the area. The local papers wanted a slogan that would identify – and unify – the entire region.

"'South-central Idaho' isn't exactly a name to run up on the flagpole and salute," wrote the *Times-News* in its Territorial Centennial edition in 1963. (The *Idaho Evening Times* and the *Twin Falls Daily News* combined later to make the *Times-News*.)

"Magic Valley" became the official nickname of the region, including Twin Falls, Cassia, Minidoka, Blaine, Lincoln, Jerome, Camas and Gooding counties.

Henry Harris: the Legendary Black Buckaroo

Headstones can be deceiving.

Southern Idaho's legendary black cowboy Henry Harris was said to have been conceived in slavery, and born in freedom. The official date of his birth is Dec. 15, 1865, seven months after the Civil War ended.

But Harris' headstone in the Twin Falls Cemetery says he was born in 1868. According to Harris' biographer Les Sweeney, he simply refused to accept his real age. Harris was 71 when he died in 1937 – or maybe older, Sweeney said. The headstone describes Harris as a "pioneer cowboy." That doesn't even come close to describing Harris' remarkable life, he said.

Harris' parents were former slaves living in Texas. Harris was born a free man, and was somewhat educated.

Harris was still young when he went to work as a servant for Texas cattleman John Sparks, who later became the governor of Nevada. Sparks took Harris with him when he moved to Nevada from Texas in 1884.

Sparks and John Tinnen, another cattleman from Texas, put together a cattle empire that spread from Wells, NV to Utah, and into southern Idaho. According to Sweeney, the Sparks and Tinnen herd numbered between 50,000 and 70,000 head of cattle.

HIDDEN HISTORY

PHOTOS COURTESY OF TWIN FALLS COUNTY HISTORICAL MUSEUM

Legendary black cowboy Henry Harris was conceived in slavery and born in freedom. Harris was inducted into the Buckaroo Hall of Fame in Winnemucca, NV in 2008, and into the National Cowboys of Color Hall of Fame in Fort Worth, TX in 2009.

Harris graduated from house boy to cow puncher. He soon became a wagon boss and foreman of the Boar's Nest, Middle Stack, and Vineyard ranches just south of the Idaho border.

Harris was a living legend, Sweeney said. Black cowboys were not common in Nevada and Idaho in those days, but a black man who was a ranch boss over white cowboys was unheard of.

In 1894, he acquired 160 acres of land southwest of present-day Salmon Falls Reservoir. In 1930, Harris bought another 35 acres near Rogerson.

The cattle ranches changed hands many times over the decades, but Harris remained loyal to his vocation until his death.

Nora Bowman, wife of Utah Construction Co. superintendent Archie Bowman, wrote about Harris' death in her book "Only the Mountains Remain."

"He knew we all liked and respected him and that he was welcome wherever he went," she wrote.

Harris was inducted into the Buckaroo Hall of Fame in Winnemucca, NV in 2008, and into the National Cowboys of Color Hall of Fame in Fort Worth in 2009.

Sleuth Finds Pistol Likely Used in Century Old Murders

Either Jim Bower or Jeff Gray — or maybe both — shot and killed Oakley sheepherders John Wilson and Daniel Cummings in 1896.

Never heard of any of them? Chances are you are not alone.

The title character of southern Idaho's best-known murder mystery was "Diamondfield Jack" Davis, an innocent man who was tried, convicted and sentenced to hang for the killings. Over the years, Davis' story has eclipsed the real story about the victims and the shooters.

Several years ago, former Idaho Rep. Max Black visited the city park in Albion, where a historical marker is dedicated to Diamondfield Jack. The story on the marker left Black hungry for more details of the crime itself.

"I couldn't find anyone who knew exactly where this took place," Black said. "Then I wondered about the court records."

Black contacted the Idaho State Historical Society and was led to a large box containing old newspaper clippings and transcripts from Davis' trial.

In mid-February 1896, Oakley sheepherder Ted Severe found his friends Wilson and Cummings shot to death in their sheep-camp wagon along Deep Creek, in the Shoshone Basin area, north of the Nevada border. Cassia County authorities estimated that the sheepherders had been dead for two weeks. Davis quickly became the one and only suspect in the deaths.

John Sparks — who later became the governor of Nevada — hired Davis to police the range claimed by the Sparks-Harrell Cattle Co.

Jeff Gray and Sparks-Harrell foreman Jim Bower, who were known to have been in the area when the shooting occurred, denied any responsibility in the murders.

Davis' trial was high profile from the beginning.

Cassia County Prosecuting Attorney John C. Rogers brought in William Borah — who would later become a U.S. senator from Idaho — and Orlando Power, a former Supreme Court Justice in Utah Territory.

Davis' defense team included future governor of Idaho James Hawley, Kirkland Perky — a former law partner of William Jennings Bryan — and future U.S. senator Will Puckett.

Davis was convicted and sentenced to hang the following year. Shortly before Davis was to face the gallows, Bower and Gray confessed to shooting the sheepherders in self defense, and Davis was given a short reprieve.

According to their depositions, Wilson attacked Bower in the camp wagon, knocking Bower down. Fearing Bower would be killed, Gray shot both Wilson and Cummings. In the scuffle, Bower was able to remove his short barrel .44 caliber Model 1878 Colt Frontiersman from its shoulder holster, and fired a few shots of his own.

Despite the confessions, Borah was not willing to concede defeat. Through appeal after appeal, Davis spent a total of six years in prison, before he was eventually pardoned and released.

Black became somewhat obsessed with the murders, trying to sort out fact from fiction. In the court papers, he found surveys of the crime scene that eventually directed him to the site.

Black solicited the aid of Hollister native Alex Kunkel to triangulate the coordinates determined by the 1896 surveys. The two located the old camp site on private property in what is now southern Twin Falls County.

With a metal detector, Black located a .44 slug wedged under a rock. It is

HIDDEN HISTORY

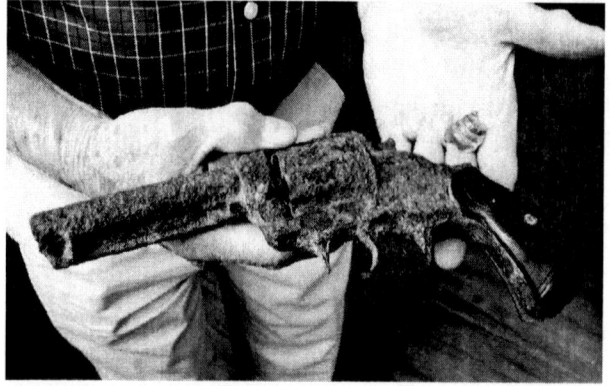

MYCHEL MATTHEWS, TIMES-NEWS
Retired Idaho Rep. Max Black holds a short barrel .44 caliber Model 1878 Colt Frontiersman pistol, possibly owned by James Bower in 1896. Note the missing sight at the end of the barrel, which indicates that the pistol was shoulder holstered.

PHOTO COURTESY OF TWIN FALLS COUNTY HISTORICAL MUSEUM
Seated in this photo by an unknown photographer is Jeff Gray, who confessed to killing Oakley sheepherders John Wilson and Danial Cummings in 1896. Standing is Charles Henderson Hewitt, uncle of Twin Falls celebrity centenarian Dorothy Custer, who died in 2015 just short of her 104th birthday.

believed to be the missing slug that was shot through a saddle hanging on a large sagebrush in the camp. Black believes the slug was shot from Bower's pistol, which according to Bower's deposition, was lost in the desert after the shooting.

Black took the slug to a Boise firearms expert to verify its age and caliber. After Black explained the story of the slug, the man told Black that he had purchased a short barrel .44 caliber Model 1878 Colt Frontiersman from a man who had found the rusted pistol in the desert near the area Black had described. The sight had been filed off the pistol, which was then a common revision to shoulder-holstered pistols like Bower's.

The Staircase at Kiwanis Nook

An elaborate rock staircase near Shoshone Falls makes an appearance every couple of decades, only to disappear under a thick overgrowth of vegetation. The staircase, which follows a trickle of spring water down the Snake River Canyon's south rim at Shoshone Falls, is known as "Kiwanis Nook."
In late April 2013, 90 volunteers from the Church of Jesus Christ of Latter-day Saints chopped through the vines and cleared the brush that had claimed the staircase. The group also tackled the intersecting Centennial Trail, which had become tangled in overgrowth.
"While we were unearthing the stairs, the kids joked that we were unearthing

PHOTO COURTESY OF TRENT LAMARCHE
Volunteers from teh Church of Jesus Christ of Latter-day Saints worked to reclaim the staircase at "Kiwanis Nook" west of Shoshone Falls. To reach the stairs, hike a short distance up the Centennial Trail. The stairs are just east of the second Shoshone Falls overlook.

an ancient civilization," said Trent LaMarche, a councilman with the church's Twin Falls South Stake.

It isn't ancient, but the staircase at Shoshone Falls Park was made so long ago that its origin is not readily known today.

According to Dennis Bowyer, director of the Twin Falls Parks and Recreation Department, the rock staircase was probably built during the Great Depression, as part of a larger project undertaken at the park by the Civilian Conservation Corps or the Works Progress Administration.

Before that, the staircase was part of an elaborate trail system that crisscrossed the park.

The city of Twin Falls has owned the land southwest of Shoshone Falls since the early 1930s, Bowyer said. Franklin J. and Martha Adams gave the city 68 acres for a park in 1932, and the following year, the state of Idaho donated several hundred acres west of the Adams property.

HIDDEN HISTORY

When built, the rock staircase descended from the old rim road – today's Centennial Trail – to a rock ledge overlooking the Snake River. The nook, which includes the staircase and several picnic areas, had been cleared out several times over the years by the Kiwanis Club, said long-time club member David Mead.

"There were no railings way back when," said Mead, "and the stairs were rather dangerous."

The church volunteers worked their way down two flights of stairs, clearing mud and replacing rocks as they went. The upper path is still a little rough in places, but navigable.

The bottom stairs and overlook are gone — erased by time. But it is not likely that nature will reclaim the staircase any time soon.

"We'd like to see the staircase brought back to how it looked in its Glory Days," Bowyer said.

Headstones are all that Remain of Artesian City

A few headstones in the Artesian City Cemetery are the only evidence that a town ever existed here.

Cattleman James E. Bower is credited with settling the area where Dry Creek flows out of the South Hills in Cassia County and into Twin Falls County on its way to the Snake River.

Bower came to Idaho in 1873 with a large herd of A.J. Harrell's cattle, and settled in the Shoshone Basin just north of the Nevada border. By 1876, Harrell claimed some 800 acres of homestead and desert land at the mouth of Dry Creek Canyon.

According to the memoirs of long time Murtaugh resident Oliver Johnson, Bower was described as "a small man with beady eyes and had a mean reputation typical of hard men who settled the West."

Locally, Bower was known to have killed more than a few men, according to Johnson.

Bower confessed to being an accomplice in the 1895 murder of two Oakley sheep herders, John Wilson and Daniel Cummings. His confession eventually led to the pardon and release of the infamous "Diamondfield" Jack Davis. But that's another story.

In 1895, Bower drilled two water wells for his livestock near his home just east of Dry Creek. But instead of potable water, Bower hit a pocket of 110-degree water with seemingly endless potential.

By 1909, Bower sold off a large portion of his property and two dozen families

PHOTO COURTESY OF CLARENCE E. BISBEE; RESTORED BY BLIP PRINTERS
Seen in this restored C.E. Bisbee photo are two artesian wells on James Bower's proeprty at Artesian City, south of Murtaugh. The wells were later developed into a health spa known as Artesian Natatorium.

moved into the area. That year, Idaho Real Estate and Produce Co. announced the development of Artesian City on 560 acres of former Bower property, at that time owned by Frank Somsen.

Artesian opened in September 1909, with the promise of electricity, a health spa and retreat, and frost-free irrigation for fruit orchards—all from the artesian water.

Folks quickly established a general store, a school, a hotel, a livery stable, a dance hall, a post office and a cemetery.

The town was short lived.

The post office shut down in 1913. An inter-urban railroad that was to run from the Murtaugh train depot to Artesian and on to Oakley, never got past the planning stage.

But the town had one success.

In its heyday, the Artesian Natatorium - the "Nat," for short - was the favorite hot springs resort in the Magic Valley. The Nat—which consisted of two indoor swimming pools—opened in April 1916.

Promoters invited the public to visit Artesian, where "the air is pure (and) the climate is delightful."

The Nat operated several decades. Some say the hot springs dried up when irrigation wells were drilled in the area. Others say interest in the spa waned, and it went out of business. The artesian wells were capped and the townsite has been reclaimed by farmland.

PHOTO COURTESY OF CLARENCE E. BISBEE; RESTORED BY BLIP PRINTERS

The Artesian Natatorium was a popular hot springs resort from 1916 to 1925. The Nat was located in Cassia County, across the county line from Artesian City, south of Murtaugh Lake.

The Wizard of Kimberly Road

Some say the man was a genius. Others say he was an ordinary fellow who did extraordinary things when he set his mind to it.
Either way, Norman Herrett was a man who inspired many lives.
Herrett taught school for some 20 years before building his legacy, the Herrett Arts and Science Center, on Kimberly Road, just east of Blue Lakes Boulevard. In 1946, Herrett turned a hobby of collecting rocks into a business of selling polished agate when he opened Herrett Manufacturing Jewelers. Herrett and his wife Lillie lived in the back of the building, part of which still stands today. With income from his jewelry store, Herrett built a planetarium and observatory onto the store. In his spare time, he made telescopes from scratch, using irrigation pipe and various odds and ends to bring his creations to life.
"Norm was a wizard, a magician and a visionary," said Don Hite, who worked at the planetarium in his youth. "But most importantly, he was very human."
And he understood how kids learn.
Herrett knew that "kids would listen to other kids more readily than they would listen to adults," Hite said. So in the 1950s, Herrett designed a program

PHOTO COURTESY OF DON HITE
The Herrett Arts and Science Center sat on the south side of Kimberly Road, just east of Blue Lakes Boulevard. The planetarium and observatory dome are seen on the right in this photo from the 1960s. Norman Herrett's jewelry store is on the right, and the Herrett museum is in the center. Portions of the complex still stand today.

of kids teaching kids at the planetarium. Hite and other student lecturers from the Magic Valley took countless groups of school children on trips through the solar system in a planetarium that had sound effects and vibrating seats that simulated a ride in a rocket ship.

PHOTO COURTESY OF DON HITE
Norman Herrett is seen at the controls of his planetarium, which he designed and built from scratch.

"As soon as the lights came down, the trip became a most unearthly experience," Hite said. "Norm really knew how to reach out and grab kids."

Busloads of students from as far away as Mountain Home and Burley flocked to the planetarium. Hite estimates that 10,000 kids went through the planetarium each year.

Eventually, a museum that housed prehistoric artifacts was built onto the complex.

In 1972, Herrett agreed to donate his collections to the College of Southern Idaho if the college agreed to build a place to house them. A planetarium and observatory were also planned.

And the Herrett Center for Arts and Sciences was born.

Hites memories of Norman Herrett can be read online by visiting www.donhite.com/herrett.

"Herrett was simply larger than life," Hite said.

Buildings Lost Over the Years

Many century-old buildings have been preserved in the historic downtown district. But unfortunately, several magnificent buildings have been lost over the years.

One of the first buildings constructed in the original townsite of Twin Falls was the Hotel Perrine, located in the center of town on the west corner of Shoshone and Main.

Sources debate the identity of the designer of the building. Some say the hotel was designed by planner E.L. Masqueray, the man responsible for the diagonal orientation of the townsite's streets. Others say it was designed by architect J. Flood Walker. Both men were associated with the 1904 Louisiana Purchase Exposition in St. Louis.

The grand hotel opened in December 1905.

The three-story building was constructed in a U shape, with a second-story balcony facing Main. The hotel occupied the second and third floors, while the ground floor was filled with businesses.

The hotel was a model of prosperity in its day. It featured an atrium and a formal dining room. Each hotel room had running water, electric lights, steam heat and a telephone.

A steam engine-driven Case threshing machine behind the hotel ran an Edison generator, producing enough electricity to power the hotel and businesses in several blocks each direction.

Twin Falls grew rapidly over the next few years.

By 1910, Bickel and Lincoln schools were bursting at the seams. Across Shoshone Street from the city park, a new school was built next to the courthouse, which was also under construction. Twin Falls High School opened in February 1912. By the 1912-1913 school year, there were more than 1,700 students enrolled in the new school. It was hailed as the best equipped high school in the Northwest. By 1921, the school accommodated both senior and junior high school students. In 1925, Vera C. O'Leary was appointed principal of the junior high school students.

PHOTO COURTESY OF CLARENCE E. BISBEE; RESTORED BY BLIP PRINTERS
Three-time presidential candidate William Jennings Bryan is seen speaking to a crowd outside the Hotel Perrine in September 1907. The Twin Falls landmark - located on the west corner of Shoshone and Main - was demolished in 1968.

When high school students were moved to the new high school on Filer Avenue East in 1952, the old school became known as Twin Falls Junior High School. In 1963, the junior high was renamed Vera C. O'Leary Junior High School in honor of O'Leary, who, due to declining health, was unable to continue as principal.

PHOTO COURTESY OF CLARENCE E. BISBEE; RESTORED BY BLIP PRINTERS
Twin Falls High School, built in 1911, is seen the following year standing next to the courthouse on Shoshone Street North.

HIDDEN HISTORY

Over the years, the building deteriorated faster than it could be repaired. Eventually, the third floor was condemned.

For several semesters during 1976 and 1977, the building was closed by the fire department. Junior and high school students alike attended the newer building in double shifts, until a sprinkler system could be installed inside O'Leary.

The old building limped along until 1978, when it was replaced by a new O'Leary Junior High on Elizabeth Boulevard.

The Hotel Perrine survived until 1968, when the building was replaced with a new bank. The old Twin Falls High School was demolished in 1980 to make way for the county judicial building and jail.

The Tragic Tale of Lew and Ella Newton

Lew Newton tossed around a lot of bones in his trade, but it would be his own bones that would give a name to a distinct butte east of Twin Falls.

Newton was a butcher from Nevada. Sometime around 1880, he came to Idaho and met Ella O'Neil in the mining town of Atlanta.

Newton married Ella — who was said to be a refined and possibly wealthy woman — and the two moved to the Wood River Valley. Newton opened a butcher shop, and Ella ran a restaurant and lodge.

Money was plentiful in the local mining camps, and gambling was a common pastime. It wasn't long before Newton joined the others at the poker tables.

Newton soon gave up his butcher shop to become a professional gambler. He left his wife at home in Bellevue and moved to the new railroad town of Shoshone.

Ella became destitute and was forced to pawn some of her jewelry to make ends meet. In January 1883, the Newton home burned down. Ella died in the fire.

According to newspaper reports, shots were heard in the house moments before the fire began. It was speculated that Ella committed suicide or that she was murdered for her jewelry.

Newton was devastated by his wife's death. After Ella's funeral, Newton returned, penniless, to Shoshone.

In Shoshone, Newton heard that a $50 reward had been offered for the return of a large herd of mules stolen from a local freight company.

Meanwhile, a gang of horse thieves had taken up residence in Devil's Corral, a rugged canyon area on the north side of the Snake River a few miles upstream from Shoshone Falls.

Newton assumed that the outlaws at Devil's Corral had the missing mules.

PHOTO COURTESY OF CLARENCE E. BISBEE, TWIN FALLS COUNTY HISTORICAL MUSEUM
Sentinel Gate at Devils Corral is seen in this Clarence E. Bisbee photo.

Determined to earn the reward money, he borrowed a horse and saddle, and rode off in search of the herd.
He never returned.
A year later, a man's remains were discovered on a butte five miles east of Devil's Corral. The man had been shot through the chest and buried in a shallow grave. Coyotes had scattered his remains over the hillside.
The last letter Ella Newton wrote to her husband was discovered in the man's pocket, and the area would become known as Skeleton Butte.

Early Landowners Weren't Always Homesteaders

Over the years, Hollywood has created dramatic images of homesteaders racing covered wagons across acres of empty prairies to claim free land from the government. That may have happened in certain rare instances, but never here.
That's not to say that there weren't homesteads in this desert — just that much of the land here wasn't worth giving away. Not without water, in any case.
Herman Stricker homesteaded on Rock Creek south of present-day Hansen.

HIDDEN HISTORY

Charles Walgamott homesteaded at Shoshone Falls. And I.B. Perrine homesteaded at Blue Lakes in the Snake River Canyon.

Each of these homesteaders had one thing in common: a source of irrigation water they could rely on.

The Homestead Act of 1862 was intended to settle the West. With a little ambition, almost anyone could stake a claim on 160 acres of federal land and make it his in five years' time.

The Homestead Act was a success in states with adequate rainfall. Between 1862 and 1904, 500 million acres of federal land was dispersed by the General Land Office.

But choice property was claimed quickly, leaving vast areas of desert land still up for grabs, including most of what would become the Magic Valley.

Several decades went by, and the federal government realized the Homestead Act had fallen short of expectations in arid western states.

While the Homestead Act represented a contract between the federal government and individual landowners, the Carey Act represented a contract between the government and private corporations that were able to take on

PHOTO COURTESY OF CLARENCE E. BISBEE, TWIN FALLS COUNTY HISTORICAL MUSEUM
The Salmon Dam, west of Hollister, was one of several dams in the area constructed under the Carey Act more than 100 years ago. The dam is on the National Register of Historic Places.

such large projects. The act allowed private enterprise to construct irrigation projects and develop the land for the government, then sell the accompanying irrigation water to farmers at a profit.

The largest and most successful of any Carey Act reclamation project in the United States is the Milner Dam irrigation project that irrigates nearly a half million acres in southern Idaho.

Happy Holly Brings Big Names to Town

Sixty-five years ago, a young man came to town who was bound for stardom. And with him, came a steady stream of national celebrities.

Local radio and television personality Holland Lynn Houfburg — better known as "Happy Holly" — brought to town dozens of the biggest names in country and western music during the 1950s and 1960s.

Thanks to Holly, Magic Valley music lovers needed to go only as far as the county fairgrounds to see Johnny Cash and June Carter, or Jackpot to see Roy Acuff and Minnie Pearl.

Holly's childhood dream was to become a radio man, said his younger brother, Carl Houfburg.

Growing up in Illinois, Holly was afflicted with a lung ailment that kept him from enjoying a physically active childhood, Carl said. While other boys were outside playing football or riding bikes, Holly and Carl stayed indoors playing "radio station."

At 16, Holly began his radio career as a sound technician at WBBM in Chicago. He later went to Hollywood to work as a roadie for western music and film star Gene Autry. It was during this time that Holly befriended many Nashville entertainers.

Carl — who was in the cattle business — talked Holly into moving to Idaho with him in 1950. Shortly afterward, Holly pitched an idea to KLIX-AM in Twin Falls and he was hired as the "KLIX Klodhopper" to do remote radio broadcasts across the Magic Valley.

Holly's popularity quickly spread throughout southern Idaho. He broadcast several radio programs every day, and hosted the kids' television show "KLIX Kowhand Klub" live each afternoon.

In the mid-1950s, Cactus Petes casino opened in Jackpot, Nev. To lure Idaho gamblers across the state line, Cactus Petes hired Holly to contract entertainment out of Nashville. Holly's band, the Double H Buckaroos, became Cactus Petes' house band, and performed with the likes of Roy Clark, George Jones, Kitty Wells and Slim Whitman.

HIDDEN HISTORY

Other stars that Holly brought to town included Hank Snow, Ferlin Husky, Tex Ritter, Rex Allen and Johnny Horton.

In 1958, Holly was named "Mr. Disc Jockey —USA" by the country music industry.

After Holly left to receive his award, KLIX-AM announced its plan to send a telegram to Holly in Nashville. Anyone who wanted to congratulate Holly could call into the radio station to have their name included on the telegram. The telegram was delivered to Holly on the stage, along with his award. While

VIC GRAYBEAL PHOTO COURTESY OF TWIN FALLS COUNTY HISTORICAL MUSEUM
Holland "Happy Holly" Houfburg brought music giant Johnny Horton to Twin Falls in 1960. Houfburg and his band, the Double H Buckaroos, are seen with Horton on Addison Avenue West near Grandview Drive. The band -- dressed up as British soldiers from Horton's No. 1 song, 'The Battle of New Orleans' -- "captured" Horton and hauled him to his concert at Jaycee Field.

Holly held one end of the telegram, a long list of well-wishers unfurled across the stage and into the aisle of the Grand Ole Opry. The Magic Valley star was reduced to tears.

Holly's life kept up a frenzied pace until 1970, when he shifted gears to start up the audio-visual program at the College of Southern Idaho. Holly retired from the college shortly before his death in 1983.

MYCHEL MATTHEWS

PHOTO COURTESY OF VIC GRAYBEAL, TWIN FALLS COUNTY HISTORICAL MUSEUM
Happy Holly stands second from the right, next to Roy Acuff. Also among the group of country music entertainers are George Jones and Kitty Wells, both standing at the far left.

Charlie McMaster's Horses

Some came to this new town to make their fortunes. Others brought their fortunes with them.

Charlie McMaster was a prosperous farmer and livestock dealer in Hopkins, Mo., before he brought his family to Idaho. McMaster heard about the new irrigation tract opening up in southern Idaho, when he and his wife, Della, visited her parents in Boise in 1904.

Before returning to Missouri, McMaster filed on 160 acres on Kimberly Road east of Twin Falls.

McMaster sold his land in Hopkins and filled three freight cars with personal belongings to take to his new home in Idaho. McMaster and several employees traveled by train to Shoshone, then crossed the desert to Blue Lakes where they ferried the Snake River into what was then Cassia County.

McMaster's wife and young daughter followed him west after he had a chance to get settled.

When Della McMaster reached her husband's tent near Kimberly, she was greeted with little enthusiasm.

"Dell, this is no place for you and Georgia," McMaster said. "You had better go to Boise until we have had time to make the place more fit for you to live in." But Della refused to leave. She was determined to make a home in this desert. Within months, the McMasters built a home on two lots in the 400 block of Third Avenue West in Twin Falls. McMaster and his business partner, Nick Smith, opened a livery stable nearby and purchased an additional 1,200 acres to farm.

HIDDEN HISTORY

PHOTO COURTESY OF CLARENCE E. BISBEE, TWIN FALLS COUNTY HISTORICAL MUSEUM

McMaster is best remembered for his fine saddle horses and is known to have brought the first Morgan horse into Idaho. His "Pride of Twin Falls" is seen in front of McMaster's home, which still stands on the west corner of Eden Street and Third Avenue West in Twin Falls.

McMaster and Smith began importing livestock from Iowa and Missouri — pedigreed Duroc Jersey hogs and Hereford cattle that would become the foundation for local herds.

But McMaster found his greatest joy in horseflesh.

McMaster is best remembered for his fine saddle horses, and is known to have brought the first Morgan horse into Idaho.

McMaster also brought in many hundreds of Percheron and Belgian draft horses to clear the desert of sagebrush. Most of these work horses were sold to local farmers on credit. Farmers paid McMaster for their teams after their crops were harvested.

Over the years, the McMasters continued to prosper. They had a son, Frank, in 1907, and in 1908 Charlie was elected Twin Falls county commissioner, the same year he founded Farmers Real Estate, Grain and Livestock Co.

After Charlie's death in 1936, Della found thousands of dollars' worth of unpaid notes in her husband's belongings — notes signed by local farmers who were unable to pay back their debt to McMaster.

Della gathered all the notes and set fire to them in the alley behind her house.

A Snapshot of the Idaho Territory

A century and a half ago, President Abraham Lincoln signed a Congressional act creating the territory of Idaho.

But the resulting jurisdiction hardly resembled the state we know today. Idaho in 1863 included the area that would later become Montana and most of Wyoming. The population base — mostly gold miners chasing dreams of wealth — was then located in the Clearwater region in what is now Idaho's panhandle.

PUBLIC DOMAIN
William H. Wallace is seen in his official portrait as the first governor of the Territory of Idaho.

The politics of that time would also seem foreign today. Territories had little control over their own affairs, wrote former University of Idaho professor Carlos A. Schwantes in his book "In Mountain Shadows." Territories were controlled by the federal government and officiated by appointees of the president.

"Idaho's territorial governors were for the most part an odd lot of scheming or incompetent carpetbag politicians who seemed to serve the territory best by leaving it, or not arriving at all," Schwantes wrote.

There was at least one exception to this generalization, says Keith Petersen, historian with the Idaho State Historical Society.

"There were some colorful characters in the territorial government," Petersen said, but William H. Wallace was not one of them. Wallace, an old friend of Lincoln, was appointed Idaho's first territorial governor.

Before then, Wallace was a Washington territorial delegate to Congress from Puget Sound, and had a genuine interest in the West, Petersen said. During this time, Wallace was instrumental in creating the territory of Idaho and consequently appointed governor.

It is not known how good of a governor Wallace could have been, since he served for less than a year before being elected to Congress once again.

Lincoln appointed Caleb Lyon as the second governor in 1864. Lyon signed legislation to move the capitol from Lewiston to Boise soon after arriving in the territory, creating a bitter conflict between residents of northern Idaho and the burgeoning region of southern Idaho.

Lewiston residents considered the move illegal. Armed guards prevented Boise residents from moving the territorial seal and archives from Lewiston, and Lyon slipped quietly out of town.

Acting governor, Territorial Secretary Clinton Dewitt Smith, managed to move the seal and archives to Boise in 1865. But seven months after replacing Lyon, Smith drank himself to death.

Later, Governor Horace Gilson looted the territorial treasury of $41,000 before leaving the country.

Meanwhile, the size of the new territory proved too large to handle. In 1864, the Montana territory was carved out of the northeast corner of Idaho territory, and in 1866, Wyoming territory was created, leaving Idaho with its present-day boundaries.

'Owyhee' Means Hawaii

Say "Hawaii" out loud. Now say it again, this time without pronouncing the "H."

The Hawaiian Islands were discovered by British Capt. James Cook in 1777. Cook named Hawaii "Sandwich Islands" after the Earl of Sandwich, but the name did not stick for long.

After Cook left Hawaii, he explored and mapped the northern Pacific coastline to the Bering Strait, looking for the famed "Northwest Passage" that would connect the Pacific and Atlantic oceans in the Arctic. Failing to find the Northwest Passage, Cook returned to Hawaii, where he was killed by natives in 1779.

From then until the Panama Canal was completed in 1914, Hawaii was a regular stop for trade ships that sailed around Cape Horn. In the years after Cook's death, many Hawaiians boarded ships as crew members or fur trappers. The fur trade with China was huge at the turn of the 19th century. John Jacob Astor — the richest man in America at the time — wanted to capitalize on the fur industry in the Pacific Northwest, but there were no ports along its coast. Astor thought that he could gain control over the fur trade by establishing a fort at the mouth of the Columbia River. In 1810, Astor hired Wilson Price Hunt to lead an expedition over uncharted territory west of St. Louis to Ft. Astoria.

In 1811, Hunt and his group were the first Euro-Americans to travel through what would become southern Idaho.

Astor's ownership of Ft. Astoria was short-lived. During the War of 1812, Astor sold the fort to the British-owned North West Co., and Ft. Astoria then became Ft. George.

Donald Mackenzie, one of the explorers in the Hunt party, returned to Idaho in 1818 with a group of fur trappers that included three natives from Hawaii — or Owyhee, which was the early, phonetic spelling of Hawaii. The

three Hawaiians left Mackenzie's group during the winter of 1819-1820, and disappeared into the mountains, never to be seen again.
The fate of the men is not known, but most historians assume they were killed by Indians.
In honor of the men, the area where the men disappeared was became known as "Owyhee."

How the Malad River Got Its Name

The Malad River bears one of the oldest names in the Magic Valley, christened by one of the first white men to enter southern Idaho.
Donald Mackenzie was an Astorian and part of the Wilson Price Hunt expedition that met with disaster on the Snake River in eastern Twin Falls County some 200 years ago. After exploring the Snake River Canyon for a few days, Mackenzie and a small group of men headed north on foot, in search of Ft. Astoria at the mouth of the Columbia River.
Local historian Jim Gentry says Mackenzie's exact route north is unknown. But on that trip, he probably never saw the Malad River Gorge, which gives the river its tourist-attraction status today.
"Mackenzie would have thought that the river impeded his travel," Gentry said. From the Snake River near today's Milner Dam, Mackenzie's group headed north in early November 1811. His group arrived at Astoria in January 1812, a month ahead of Hunt and the rest of the Astorians.
Mackenzie returned to southern Idaho in 1818, as a part of the British-owned North West Co.
The next year, Mackenzie's group of trappers became ill after eating beaver meat while camped on the banks of the river that Mackenzie named "Malad" — meaning "sick" in French.
In his "Reminiscences of Early Days Volume II," pioneer author Charles Walgamott claims the beaver in the Malad River had gained a solid reputation for sickening trappers.
Alexander Ross and his men had an experience similar to Mackenzie's in 1824, and assumed the beaver had been dining on the roots of some poisonous plant growing along the stream. Ross named the stream "Riviere Malades," said Walgamott. John Work also noticed dead fish in the stream in 1830, and he named it "Sickly River."
Walgamott, who came to Idaho from Iowa in 1875, speculated that it was the root of the poisonous water hemlock that the beaver were eating that was sickening those who ate the meat.

HIDDEN HISTORY

PHOTO COURTESY OF CLARENCE E. BISBEE, TWIN FALLS COUNTY HISTORICAL MUSEUM
The Malad River, seen here as it winds its way through the Malad River Gorge, was named by North West Co. trapper Donald Mackenzie in 1819.

The Malad River starts near Gooding, where the Big Wood River and the Little Wood River converge. From there, it travels 12 miles to the Snake River near Hagerman. The Malad River Gorge is 250 feet deep and nearly three miles long. Interstate 84 crosses the Malad River Gorge near Tuttle.

Was Dowdle Bill Really a Scoundrel?

William F. Dowdle has always been portrayed as a no-good, thievin' drunk. Dowdle was caught trying to sell a stolen horse at Rock Creek Stage Stop in 1875 and was jailed for days underground in a cellar behind Stricker Store. Passersby mocked him, chanting "Dowdle Bill" outside his cell. He was convicted of theft and sentenced to several years in the territorial prison. The whole time he was in prison, he plotted revenge against the men who captured him. Blood would run in the streets, Dowdle promised.
Or so the story goes.
Dowdle did return to the stage stop after his release from prison — supposedly

to kill stage stop operator Charles Trotter and cowboy E.D. Wilson. But, when Dowdle got there, one of the men was sick in bed and the other was out of town.

Disappointed, Dowdle spent the rest of the day drinking in the saloon.

After some time, Dowdle stepped out of the saloon and started shooting at people. He narrowly missed hitting Charlie Walgamott, Trotter's brother-in-law and clerk at the general store.

Walgamott returned fire, killing Dowdle.

Dowdle's body was paraded around town as people rejoiced and sang. Travelers waiting in a stagecoach were appalled at the barbaric nature displayed by Rock Creek locals.

This is what legends are made of, said Ted Dunaski, who is married to Dowdle's great-great niece Lori.

Dunaski has a hard time reconciling the story with what he knows about Dowdle.

Dowdle once risked his own life to save an Indian boy during a massacre, proving that Dowdle was not a "complete scoundrel," Dunaski said.

Dunaski says he is looking for clues to who Dowdle was and how he ended up at Rock Creek.

Dowdle was born in Alabama in 1838. His family converted to Mormonism, and was one of the first Mormon families to move west. Dowdle was a cook by trade and worked for a freight company.

Dowdle — or at least part of him — is buried at a small cemetery just west of Stricker Ranch, south of Hansen. A grave-robbing incident decades ago may have resulted in a separate interment for part of his remains.

PHOTO COURTESY OF TWIN FALLS COUNTY HISTORICAL MUSEUM
Cowboys are seen at Stricker Ranch, near the old town of Rock Creek.

HIDDEN HISTORY

Canal Water Was Used for More than Irrigation

Since the early 1960s, winters have been a little easier on canal company workers.

Before then, workers spent the winters keeping the canal system free of ice — not so farmers could irrigate, but so that folks in Twin Falls could have drinking water.

"Running winter water was a costly and miserable task," wrote Al Peters, who served as Twin Falls Canal Co. general manager for almost 30 years.

In his memoirs, Peters cited one employee who lost his sight and one hand when he attempted to throw a stick of dynamite on an ice jam.

Besides accidents, there was "much suffering from the exposure to the cold and icy waters," Peters wrote.

Drinking water for early residents first came from Rock Creek, south of town. But by 1905, the demand for water surpassed the supply. The Twin Falls Waterworks Co. then contracted the new canal company to provide water for the town.

Townsfolk weren't the only ones who needed domestic water. Farmers and ranchers on the Twin Falls irrigation tract needed water for their homes and livestock yearround.

Since water wells were scarce then, the canal company encouraged those on the tract to dig cisterns to store water from the canal. Most cisterns were 10 feet deep and eight feet in diameter.

Water quality issues surfaced nearly immediately. Canal water came from the Snake River at Milner Dam, some 25 miles east of Twin Falls, and with it came fish, frogs and sediment.

In 1908, the *Twin Falls News* stated that with fresh water sources available, "there is no reason we should drink mud." In 1912, Twin Falls residents voted to establish a municipal water system that improved water pressure, but not water quality.

In 1918, voters approved a new water system and an infiltration plant opened south of town in 1919.

During the next two decades, the canal company dug seepage tunnels and thousands of drainage wells on the tract. At the same time, domestic water wells were dug where needed.

The canal company continued to supply water to Twin Falls, but not willingly. In the 1930s, an effort was made to shut down the canal system during the winter to save water reserves, but Twin Falls objected. It took another 30 years before the city developed an independent water supply and the canal company was able to halt the delivery of water during the winter.

PHOTOS COURTESY OF TWIN FALLS CANAL CO.
Canal workers break up ice jams on the Twin Falls canal system.

Not-so-funny Money

A $10 bill issued by the First National Bank of Twin Falls and signed by I.B. Perrine: Legal currency? Or Monopoly money — Magic Valley edition?
It's no joke, said Randy Perrine, great-grandson of the founder of Twin Falls. A photograph of the bill circulated town on May's page in First Federal Bank's 2013 calendar, courtesy of Perrine.
Perrine doesn't own the bill, but he does own a photo of it. Perrine loaned the photo negative to Bill Nichols, owner of BLIP Printers, to scan for the calendar. The bill is part of the 1902 "Red Seal" national currency series, issued in 1905. The bill, worth $10 in 1905, is still legal tender and worth $10 at any bank today, said Manning Garrett, owner of Old Currency LLC in South Carolina. But a private collector would have to pay around $15,000 to own it, Garrett said.
The bill in the photograph is especially valuable because of the number "1" printed under the photo of President William McKinley, he said. The number indicates that the bill came from the first page of the printing, which would be pulled out of circulation for a keepsake by the bank president.
I.B. Perrine started the First National Bank in 1905 with $25,000 in capital. He paid $3,000 for a building lot for the bank at the northeast corner of Main and Shoshone in Twin Falls. Key Bank stands at the corner now.
To nationalize the bank, Perrine bought bonds deposited with the U.S. Treasury. In exchange, the bank received national currency in $10 and $20 bills printed in Washington, D.C., and signed by the Treasurer of the United States. A $10 bill in 1905 would be worth $241 today.

HIDDEN HISTORY

PHOTO COURTESY OF RANDY PERRINE
This $10 bill is part of the 1902 "Red Seal" national currency series, issued in 1905, and signed by I.B. Perrine.

When issued by the bank, each bill would be signed by a bank cashier and bank president Perrine.

Only national banks could issue currency; state banks could not, said Garrett. "Every little town had its own bank back then," said local historian Jim Gentry. Most of the banks in the Magic Valley closed either during the agricultural depression after World War I, or later during the Great Depression, Gentry said.

The First National Bank closed in December 1931, 10 days after Twin Falls National Bank closed. Twin Falls Bank and Trust was the only bank left operating for a time.

PHOTO COURTESY OF CLARENCE E. BISBEE, TWIN FALLS COUNTY HISTORICAL MUSEUM
A wagonload of clover seed, grown on the High Line Seed Farms near the community of Clover south of Buhl, is shown in front of I.B. Perrine's First National Bank of Twin Falls.

The Power Plant at Shoshone Falls

It was raised in the name of progress.
And soon, the first hydroelectric power house at Shoshone Falls, built by Twin Falls founder I.B. Perrine, could be razed in the name of progress.
"Most visitors to Shoshone Falls don't even notice the original gray building built by Perrine," Idaho Power Co. spokesman Dan Olmstead said. The power company purchased Perrine's plant in 1916 and built another power house next to the original in 1927. Dwarfed in size and production by its successor, the first power plant still produces electricity.
Idaho Power plans to salvage the historic turbines and demolish the Perrine building in order to build a 60 megawatt facility. The 1927 power plant will remain.

ASHLEY SMITH, TIMES-NEWS
The power plant on the right was built in the early 1900s by I.B. Perrine.

The two power plants stand side by side, on the north side of the river at the base of Shoshone Falls. Water is piped from the top of the falls, through the rock to the power houses below. The falling water turns large turbines in the power houses to generate electricity.
The power plants generate a total of 12 megawatts.

HIDDEN HISTORY

Perrine first talked about building a power plant at Shoshone Falls in 1900, when he persuaded Harry Hollister, from Chicago, to invest in the hydroelectric project. Perrine then filed a claim for 3,000 cubic feet per second of water from each side of the Snake River. The claims were first intended for irrigation water, then later used for the plant.

Construction of the tunnel for the pipe, or penstock, began the following year. Crews blasted rock from the base of the canyon and tunneled upward.

In August 1907, water was released into the penstock, and 500 kilowatts of electricity were produced by the power plant. A second generator was installed in 1909, increasing production to three megawatts, the same as it produces today.

"The huge turbine wheel and the massive generator revolve at top speed with a sound like the purr of a satisfied tomcat," wrote the *Twin Falls Times* when the Perrine plant came on line.

The Mormon Corridor in Idaho

It's a long way from Salt Lake City — but it would be safe to say that there are more Mormons in Oakley, per capita, than in the headquarters of the Church of Jesus Christ of Latter-day Saints.

Vast areas of the West were first occupied by cattlemen in the 1870s. But soon, Mormon families from Utah were directed by church officials to form satellite communities in neighboring territories.

This process of "colonization" by the church was repeated across the West, from southern Idaho and southwestern Wyoming, to northern Arizona and southern Nevada, creating what is now known as the Mormon Corridor.

By 1881, families from around Grantsville, Utah, were firmly planted in Oakley, which quickly became the religious center of Cassia County.

The first emigration of Mormons began in 1846, when church president Brigham Young led 148 people from Nauvoo, Ill., to present-day Salt Lake City, following the Old Oregon Trail.

Once the Mormons reached Ft. Bridger in southwestern Wyoming, the group left the Oregon Trail and took the Hastings cutoff of the California Trail to the Great Salt Lake.

After Young established a base in Utah, he created a network of colonies designed to strengthen the Mormon presence in the West.

Young personally supervised the organization of the groups as they left for their new homes. Mormon emigrants were considered lifelong missionaries, who traveled at their own expense.

The first Mormon colony in Oregon Territory was at Ft. Lemhi, near present-day Salmon, in 1855, eight years before Idaho Territory was created. Young sent 27 families to work with local Indians and convert them to Mormonism. Conflict with the Indians erupted and two missionaries were killed. The group was called back to Salt Lake and the fort was closed in 1858.

In 1860, Mormons established the town of Franklin in southeastern Idaho, which became the first permanent settlement in the state. By 1864, there were 700 Mormon settlers in the Bear Lake region.

By 1877 — when Young died — 31 Mormon settlements had been established in southern Idaho.

But Young's death did not stop the colonization process. Families continued to expand the Mormon Corridor — or as it became later known, "The Book of Mormon Belt."

In 1879, William C. Martindale from Tooele, Utah, explored the Goose Creek Valley in Cassia County, and recommended that the area be colonized. Shortly after, the migration into Oakley began.

Bisbee's Muse Arrives in Twin Falls

Jessie Robinson was quite smitten with Clarence Bisbee when she met him in 1904.

Both Nebraska natives, Jessie was just 20 years old, and Clarence was 29.

Jessie wanted to become a kindergarten teacher. Clarence — or just "Bee" as Robinson called him — dreamed of becoming a photographer.

Jessie stayed close to home and studied at the Nebraska State Normal School. Clarence enrolled in a photography school in Effingham, Ill.

While there, Clarence met Charles Diehl, publisher and editor of the *Twin Falls News*. Diehl convinced him that the new city of Twin Falls was the place to go after graduation.

In January 1906, Clarence packed his camera and took a train to Shoshone. From Shoshone, he took a stagecoach to Twin Falls.

Clarence first set up shop in a 16-by-28 tent on Main Avenue. He later moved his photography studio to a commercial building downtown.

All the while, he courted Jessie from afar, sending her photographs of the natural wonders that would be part of their life together if she would come to Idaho.

In June 1910, Clarence traveled to Nebraska to bring Jessie home to Twin Falls. They were married in Salt Lake City.

Two days later, the newlyweds were busy taking photographs of history in the

HIDDEN HISTORY

PHOTO COURTESY OF CLARENCE E. BISBEE, TWIN FALLS COUNTY HISTORICAL MUSEUM
Jessie Robinson Bisbee, wife photographer C.E. Bisbee, poses with Ezra Meeker's oxen, Dave, left, and Twist, June 17, 1910, at Twin Falls' first Flag Day celebration at Shoshone Falls.

making.

The two built a home on Walnut Street in 1911, but it soon acquired the name "Seldom Inn."

"Our business for years absorbed us both," Jessie later wrote in her journal. "Our recreation was the outdoors."

In 1914, the Bisbees hired architect E.H. Gates to build a home and studio at the corner of Second Avenue and Second Street East — now Hansen Street East. Over the door of the studio were the words "Life and Art Are One." Clarence found inspiration in Jessie, and took thousands of photographs over his lifetime.

Jessie died in 1936. Three years later, Clarence closed the business the two had built together.

He lived the rest of his life in quiet obscurity and died in 1954.

Bee and Jessie are buried side by side in the Twin Falls Cemetery.

The Legacy of Harry Barry

"Harry Barry" isn't just a clever name for a city park.

Harry Barry was a local businessman and civic leader whose life was cut short in a tragic auto accident some 60 years ago.

After the accident that took the lives of Barry and his wife Harriet, the remaining Barrys donated a portion of the family farm to the city of Twin Falls.

A monument in Harry Barry Park now stands at the intersection of Borah Avenue West and Blake Street, in memory of Harry and Harriet.

Barry was born on a farm in Pennsylvania in 1887. After he graduated from school, Barry's father farmed him out to a neighbor, who paid the Barry family $30 per month for his labor. His father allowed him to keep $2 of the monthly wage for himself.

After three years of this arrangement, Barry decided he didn't want to spend the rest of his life "looking at the south end of a horse going north," according to a short biography written by his son David in 1988.

Barry put himself through Kansas State Teachers College, and in 1914 sent his resume to the Buhl School District. He was hired as a teacher at the high school and became the town's first football coach.

Twice in the late 1920s, Barry took the Buhl High School girls' basketball team all the way to the national championship, each time missing the win by just two points.

Barry's ambition wouldn't be contained at school, even during the Great Depression. He refused to give up after his first business failed and by the mid-1930s, he owned real estate and insurance businesses, an ice cream parlor and the *Buhl Herald*, all while continuing to teach.

In 1936, Barry decided to enter politics, much to the dismay of his college sweetheart and wife, Harriet.

His father had been a Republican, "so it was only natural that he should be a Democrat," says his biography.

Barry served in the Idaho State House of Representatives, then ran for lieutenant governor in 1940. If he failed to be elected, Barry promised Harriet that he would retire from politics.

Barry lost the election and, in 1941, moved his family to Twin Falls.

The following year, Barry bought a service station and hardware store on Addison Avenue West, and later bought a lumber company across the street. He also invested in a young block manufacturing plant in Jerome called Cinder Products Co.

Barry wrote his own advertising column in the *Times-News*, ending the column each week with his slogan "Harry Barry ain't mad at nobody."

Eventually, Barry sold the service station and hardware store, but kept Harry Barry Lumber Co.

In November 1954, Harry and Harriet Barry traveled to Kansas to visit some old friends from college. While there, they decided to drive to Oklahoma to see the Will Rogers Memorial. The road was slick from rain, and an oncoming truck slid into the Barrys' car, killing all five in the car. The driver of the truck was also killed.

The Barrys are buried in the Buhl Cemetery.

After Barry's death, Harry Barry Lumber Co. merged with the block manufacturing company that he had invested in, forming Volco Inc.

Appearance is Everything

A town without trees is not a pretty sight.

Knowing that, investors in Twin Falls poured their efforts into making the young town an attractive, civilized place to live.

Early in 1905, just months after the town was platted and surveyed, nurseryman James A. Waters began planting trees. A lot of trees. In less than a year, some 4,000 saplings lined the streets of Twin Falls.

Twin Falls Investment Co. donated two blocks on the east side of Shoshone Street for a city park, which was also filled with trees.

Many of the shade trees were planted before irrigation water from the new Twin Falls canal system had reached the town. Water was hauled in from Rock Creek, and saplings were watered by hand.

By 1910, the city's irrigation ditches were well developed and the trees were thriving. Celebrating the success of the town's beautification efforts, Waters and several friends climbed one of his trees and posed for Twin Falls

PHOTO COURTESY OF CLARENCE E. BISBEE, TWIN FALLS COUNTY HISTORICAL MUSEUM

Nurseryman James A. Waters demonstrates the size and strength of this five-year-old tree in 1910 Shoshone Street East in Twin Falls. Also in the photo are Loren A. Warner, Charles Hill, Stuart Taylor, C.E. Potter, Oren Stalker, George Sprague and Mayor Carl Hahn.

photographer Clarence Bisbee. The photo was taken in front of the ticket office of Pearcy-Tabor Co. on Shoshone Street East, in March 1910.

At the base of the five-year-old tree stands Mayor Carl Hahn, a cashier at Twin Falls Bank and Trust, holding a sapling.

At the top of the tree are Waters, the owner of Twin Falls Nursery, and Loren Warner, a Twin Falls lawyer. Below Waters and Warner are Charles Hill and Stuart H. Taylor, owners of Hill and Taylor Real Estate.

The three men in the lower branches of the tree are George Sprague, Oren Stalker and C.E. Potter.

Stalker was the proprietor of Stalker's Clothing House on Eighth Avenue North, and Sprague owned Irrigated Lands Co. and operated out of the Hotel Perrine, which can be seen in the background.

The Town of Rock Creek

Yes, there was life here before I.B. Perrine and his irrigation system.

A town was born where Rock Creek pours out of the South Hills near Kelton Road at the Old Oregon Trail.

But this may not be the Rock Creek you think.

In 1863, the Rock Creek Stage Station was established by the Ben Holladay Stage and Freight Line. The Rock Creek Store was built next to the station in 1865 by James Bascom. For a short time, the store was the only trading post on the Oregon Trail between Fort Hall and Fort Boise.

German emigrant Herman Stricker bought the store from Bascom in 1876 and homesteaded the surrounding acreage on Rock Creek. The Stricker family operated the store until 1897.

A small piece of the property, now owned by the Idaho Historical Society, is known as Rock Creek Station and Stricker Homesite — or "Stricker Ranch" for short.

About 2 miles upstream from Stricker Ranch sits what little is left of the all-but-forgotten town of Rock Creek.

According to most accounts, Rock Creek began shortly after the stage and freight line came through the area. The town had a post office by 1871 and a school by 1878. By 1900, 146 people lived in the greater Rock Creek area, including those at Stricker Ranch.

The area was populated mostly by cattle ranchers and farmers.

One notable resident was John F. Hansen, originally from Denmark. Hansen moved to Idaho in 1876 after reading a published letter by local pioneer James Iverson.

HIDDEN HISTORY

"In this land of eternal sunshine lies opportunity for all in a health giving climate unequaled anywhere," Iverson said of Rock Creek.

Hansen first settled in the Oakley area, where he taught school. He later farmed near Cottonwood Creek.

Eventually, Hansen moved to Rock Creek, where he opened a store.

The town also boasted a pool hall, hotel and a candy store.

Just after the turn of the century, I.B. Perrine founded the city of Twin Falls and the Twin Falls Irrigation Tract. Soon, the railroad entered the area along the south side of the Snake River.

In 1905, a townsite was being surveyed along the railroad, 7 miles east of Twin Falls and 7 miles north of Rock Creek. Investors made Hansen an offer he couldn't refuse: If he would move his store from Rock Creek to the new town, they would name the town after him.

PHOTO COURTESY OF CLARENCE E. BISBEE, TWIN FALLS COUNTY HISTORICAL MUSEUM
The town of Rock Creek sat just north of the South Hills on what is now 3800 East, 7 miles south of Hansen. The Rock Creek Station and Stricker Ranch complex sits northwest of the old town.

Safe Roads for Washington School

A new grade school was built in 1916 on the edge of town.
Washington School was handy for families living on the outskirts of Twin Falls.

But its convenient location — at the intersection of Addison Avenue, Blue Lakes Boulevard and Shoshone Street — led to its eventual demise.

The town grew rapidly in its first dozen years, prompting the construction of Washington School just outside the city limits. Back then, Addison and Blue Lakes marked the north and east edges of town.

The school sat at the northeast corner of North Five Points, where Albertsons supermarket sits today.

As Twin Falls continued to grow, so did the traffic on the three streets in front of Washington School.

Many of the school's students needed to cross two of the streets before and after school — and many walked home for lunch at noon.

A stoplight was eventually installed at the intersection and teachers were assigned traffic duty. In 1959, the Twin Falls Police Department took over the duty.

A student safety patrol was created to assist the traffic cop at the intersection. Lynn Brandon was part of that safety patrol in 1972.

"There were no buses at Washington School when I went there," said Brandon. "We all walked to school."

The safety patrol consisted of sixth-grade students who had good grades and showed responsibility, he said.

Members of the safety patrol wore red caps and orange Sam Browne belts, and carried long poles with red flags at the end.

Every school day, morning and afternoon, the safety patrol would position themselves at each of the five corners of the intersection. The traffic cop, whom Brandon remembers only as "Johnny," would insert a key into a control box on a pole at the school corner. When turned, the key triggered the stoplights, bringing all traffic to a halt.

The student lieutenant would give the order and the safety patrol would lower their flags into the lane of oncoming traffic, while other students scurried safely across the intersection.

In 1975, Washington School was torn down and replaced by Sawtooth Elementary School in a neighborhood with less traffic.

When built, the *Twin Falls Times* called Washington School one of the most modern schools in Idaho, complete with a basement heat plant, a stage and assembly room, three storage rooms and two "toilet rooms."

The first three schools in Twin Falls — Bickel, Lincoln and the first Twin Falls High School — were two-story, red brick buildings. Washington School broke this pattern with its gray stucco walls and single-level construction. The school was built in a unique "L" shape.

High school students on Shoshone Street who could see the grade school from their building's second-floor windows dubbed Washington School "The Tombstone."

PHOTO COURTESY OF TWIN FALLS COUNTY HISTORICAL MUSEUM; RESTORED BY BLIP PRINTERS
Washington School, built in 1916, sat on the northeast corner of North Five Points, where Albertsons Supermarket is now located.

Bringing Serial Killer Lyda Southard to Justice

If it hadn't have been for one Twin Falls County sheriff's deputy, Idaho's most notorious serial killer might have gotten away with murder.

Lyda Southard — who was born 120 years ago — is said to have poisoned four husbands and a brother-in-law, all by the time she was 27.

At the time, the story of the Twin Falls woman's dirty deeds — and her eventual capture and conviction — captivated the nation. Her story still appalls and fascinates today.

Lyda's nemesis, Deputy Virgil H. Ormsby, had no idea where the evidence would take him when he was instructed to investigate the sudden death of Edward F. Meyer, foreman of I.B. Perrine's Blue Lakes Ranch.

Meyer was a likable, hard-working man. Folks in Twin Falls were shocked when he fell ill and died in September 1919.

Many were also surprised to learn that the man had secretly married a local woman who had recently returned to town. The newlyweds didn't even live together; Meyer lived at Perrine's ranch in the Snake River Canyon, and his new wife Lyda stayed in Twin Falls, in a room at the Rogerson Hotel.

Lyda left town shortly after her husband's death.

An autopsy on Meyer's remains concluded that he died of typhoid fever, but rumors of foul play circulated around town more than a year later.

The rumors began to worry Twin Falls County Prosecutor Frank L. Stephan and newly elected Sheriff E.R. Sherman. Thinking that their careers were on the line, the two assigned Deputy Ormsby to investigate Meyer's death.

Over the next few months, Ormsby backtracked through Lyda's life, putting the pieces of the puzzle together as he found them.

Lyda Meyer was well known in Twin Falls. Her father, William Trueblood, had moved his family to town from Missouri when Lyda was young. She graduated from Twin Falls High School and in 1912 married Bob Dooley, a young man who had followed her family from Missouri. After marrying Bob Dooley, Lyda gave birth to a baby girl.

In 1915, Bob's brother and business partner, Ed Dooley, who lived with them on their farm outside Twin Falls, died suddenly after taking out a life insurance policy payable to Lyda and Bob.

Then Bob Dooley died two months later, after taking out a life insurance policy payable to Lyda.

Lyda married another Twin Falls man in 1917. Shortly afterward, Lyda's 3-year-old daughter died. Distraught over her daughter's death, Lyda and her second husband, Billy McHaffie, moved from Twin Falls to Montana.

Ormsby retraced Lyda's path to Montana, where he discovered that McHaffie had died in 1918 — after taking out a life insurance policy. Unfortunately for Lyda, McHaffie had allowed his policy to lapse before his death. Lyda tried to pay the insurance premium after McHaffie died, but the payment was denied.

While investigating McHaffie's death, Ormsby discovered that Lyda had married a Billings man by the name of Harlan Lewis in the spring of 1919. Lewis died four months later.

Ormsby went after Lyda with renewed determination after confirming that Lyda collected Lewis' $10,000 life insurance policy.

Ormsby revisited the McHaffie's former home in Montana and discovered a large quantity of cut-up fly paper containing arsenic in the basement. Arsenic residue was found in a pot Lyda had used to boil the poison out of the fly paper before tainting her husband's food.

Back in Twin Falls, Sheriff Sherman arranged to have the bodies of Lyda's

HIDDEN HISTORY

PHOTO IN PUBLIC DOMAIN
Notorious serial killer Lyda Southard is seen with Twin Falls County Sheriff E.R. Sherman, right, and Deputy Virgil H. Ormsby after her capture.

victims exhumed. Arsenic was found in all but her daughter's body, and a warrant was issued for Lyda's arrest.

Ormsby continued his hunt for Lyda until he found her living in Honolulu with her fifth husband, Paul Southard, a chief petty officer in the Navy. Ormsby escorted Lyda Southard back to Twin Falls, where she was convicted of the second-degree murder of Ed Meyer in November 1921.

Ormsby died in 1929, and is buried in the Twin Falls Cemetery near Lyda's parents, daughter and husbands Meyer and McHaffie. Lyda died in 1958 and is buried across the street in Sunset Memorial Park.

The Conviction and Escape of Lyda Southard

She claimed she wasn't a monster, but a jury of her peers disagreed.
Lyda Southard, the Twin Falls woman who is said to have killed four husbands and a brother-in-law over the course of five years, maintained her innocence to the day she died.
Charged with the poisoning of the five men, Lyda denied killing anyone. The men died of typhoid fever, Lyda said on the witness stand in the Twin Falls County courtroom.
Lyda — who was born Anna Eliza Trueblood in 1892 — claimed to be a typhoid-carrier.
The 1921 murder trial, which was covered by the *New York Times*, stunned the nation. The motive, prosecutors said, was the men's life insurance money. Although arsenic had been found in the exhumed remains of all five men, there was no evidence directly linking Lyda to any of the deaths. Knowing the evidence against Lyda was circumstantial, Twin Falls County Attorney Frank L.

Stephan brought in Idaho State Attorney General Roy L. Black to assist in the prosecution.

Attorneys from the Twin Falls law firm of Guthrie and Mills represented Lyda. Judge William Babcock presided.

After a lengthy trial, Lyda was found guilty of the second-degree murder of her fourth husband, Edward F. Meyer, foreman of I.B. Perrine's Blue Lakes Ranch. In November 1921, Lyda—known by then as "Lady Bluebeard" — was sentenced to 10 years to life in prison.

Lyda was moved from her jail cell on the fourth floor of the Twin Falls County Courthouse to the state penitentiary in Boise. She occupied one of the few cells in the women's quarters of the old pen until her escape a decade later.

Lyda managed to charm prison trusty David Minton, a machinist imprisoned for theft, about a year before he was released. Minton constructed two metal rose trellises in the prison workshop. Lyda was allowed to plant rose bushes just outside her cell window and used the trellises to train the roses up the prison wall.

Soon after his release, Minton purchased a car from a dealership in Boise, and on the night of May 4, 1931, waited for Lyda outside the prison. That night, Lyda

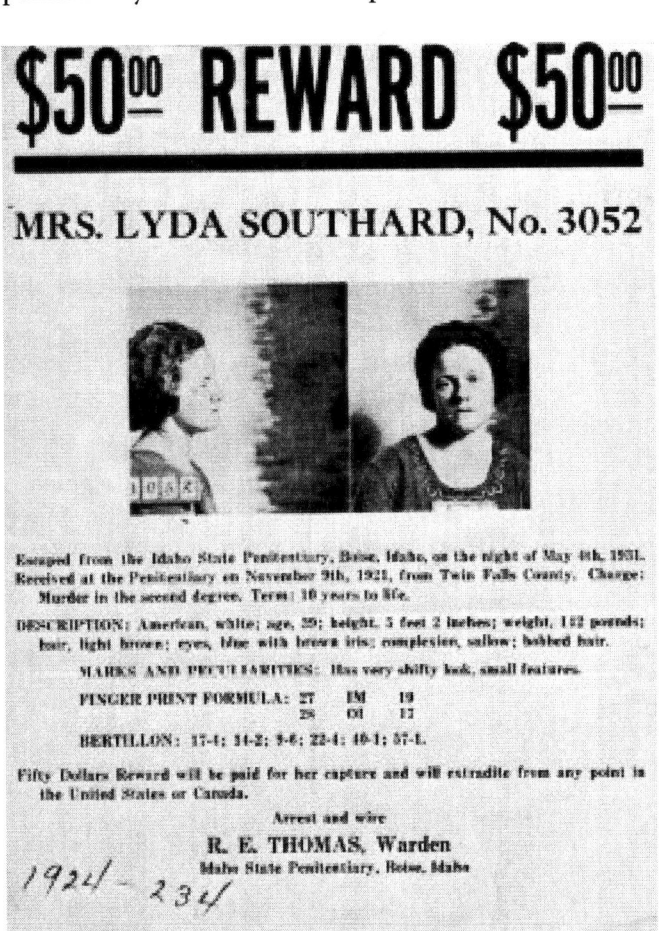

PHOTO IN PUBLIC DOMAIN
A reward for $50 was offered in 1931 for the capture of Twin Falls serial killer Lyda Southard after she escaped from the Idaho State Penitentiary in Boise.

removed a bar from her cell window and wiggled through the narrow opening. She attached the bottom of one rose trellis to the top of the other to form a ladder, then using the ladder, climbed over the prison wall. Using a garden hose and a rope made of braided bed sheets, Lyda eased herself to the ground outside the prison wall.

Minton and Lyda drove to Colorado, where they parted ways. Police caught up to Minton — who eventually disclosed Lyda's location in Denver — and returned him to Idaho.

Lyda, who had since married her sixth husband, continued to elude police. Finally, with the help of her new husband, police captured Lyda on July 30, 1932. Harry Whitlock soon had his marriage to Lyda annulled.

Lyda was returned to her cell in the Idaho State Penitentiary, and remained there until she was paroled in October 1941. She lived in Oregon and Utah, and eventually married her seventh husband, Hal Shaw, who disappeared several years later.

Lyda died of a heart attack in 1958 in Salt Lake City. She is buried in Twin Falls at Sunset Memorial Park under the name Anna E. Shaw.

The White Elephant in the City Park

Folks in early Twin Falls loved a good celebration. And, for a proper celebration, the young town needed a good band with a place to perform. The Twin Falls Municipal Band was an integral part of the community from the beginning, and band members marched down Shoshone Street every chance they got. The band gathered at city baseball games, and the bass drum sounded with every Twin Falls Cowboy home run.

By 1908, the need for a serious musical venue was apparent. Twin Falls had grown into a good-sized community, and the town began to talk about building a bandstand for concerts in the city park.

Plans for a new bandstand were drawn and local carpenters offered to donate their labor as long as the band agreed to purchase the needed materials. But that's when things went awry.

Builders inflated the cost of the materials for the bandstand until the total price tag rose to $1,800 by the time it was built in 1910. According to early newspaper accounts, the band "worked like the devil" to pay off the debt. When finished, the bandstand looked good — a lovely example of early 20th century architecture.

But as charming as it was, the bandstand itself was useless. The acoustics were terrible, and the band ended up sitting in front of the bandstand when playing for a crowd.

For the next 25 years, the failed bandstand lived its life as a gazebo. Finally, the town had enough of the white elephant in the park. The bandstand was torn down and Twin Falls architect Ernest H. Gates went to work creating a design for a new bandshell.

The city of Twin Falls paid for materials, and labor was provided by three dozen men paid through the Idaho Employment Relief Administration, the state equivalent of President Franklin Delano Roosevelt's Federal Emergency Relief Administration.

In the end, the new bandshell — which was described as a "permanent structure of beauty and usefulness" — cost the city only $700.

An estimated 800 tons of basalt rock from the Snake River rim and 10 tons of concrete was used to build the bandshell, which still stands in the city park today.

PHOTO COURTESY OF CLARENCE E. BISBEE, TWIN FALLS COUNTY HISTORICAL MUSEUM
A bandstand, far left, was built in 1910 in City Park. Acoustics were so bad in the bandstand, musicians stood on the lawn in front of the bandstand to play.

HIDDEN HISTORY

Mike's Cabin Burns in Cave Canyon Fire

Eighty years ago, Mike built a cabin.

In a 2012 fire, Mike's Cabin burned down.

To the Bureau of Land Management, Mike's Cabin was an unfortunate casualty of the recent Cave Canyon fire — an irreplaceable cultural resource that had yet to be recognized.

"I don't know why Mike's Cabin had never been recorded," said Suzann Henrikson, archaeologist with the Bureau of Land Management in Burley. Henrikson had recently begun the process to list the property on the National Register of Historic Places. Her survey crew was geared up to inspect the property this summer, until fire swept through the area.

Mike's Cabin represented a long-gone era in southern Idaho's history. Henrikson said Mike gained title to the land sometime around 1930, possibly through the Desert Land Act. The land is now part of BLM ground in the hills south of Murtaugh, just outside the National Forest Service in western Cassia County.

Although Mike's Cabin was a well-known landmark for decades, few people today know who Mike was.

"That Mike was quite a character," said Stanley Barkes, Mike's great-great nephew.

"His name was Oriel Randell," Barkes explained. "But everyone knew him as Mike. I don't know where the name 'Mike' came from."

Barkes was saddened to hear that the Cave Canyon fire had consumed Mike's Cabin. Mike built the cabin with timber from his property using an ax and a crosscut saw, when he was just 25. He used the cabin as a base camp for grazing livestock. Whisky Springs, the site of a Prohibition-era moonshine still, is just a couple miles away.

Mike's Cabin wasn't just Mike's cabin, Barkes said. It was everybody's cabin. Over the decades, countless names and initials of cabin visitors were carved in its logs. Mike's Cabin had become a safe respite for cattlemen, sheepherders, hunters and hikers alike.

After Mike sold the property, the cabin eventually fell into a state of disrepair, Barkes said. The sod roof fell in and the walls were falling down. An outhouse and barn are long gone. Now, the BLM will rely on building footprints and aerial photographs to document Mike's Cabin's existence for future generations.

"The fire took everything," said Henrikson, who visited the site in 2012. "Everything but a metal bed frame."

The Perrine Monuments at Bryan Point

On the Snake River Canyon rim overlooking Blue Lakes Country Club, stand the remnants of once-towering rock monuments built by three-time United States presidential candidate William Jennings Bryan.

The monuments were built in 1907, 10 years after Bryan befriended Magic Valley business magnate Ira Burton Perrine.

Two of the monuments were built in honor of Perrine and his wife, Hortense, said Randy Perrine, great-grandson of the couple. The third monument was for Bryan himself.

But a 1906 photograph taken by Clarence Bisbee shows — not three — but six rock monuments towering above the canyon, puzzling Randy Perrine and historians alike.

Randy, who grew up in the canyon, owns some 40 acres of the original Perrine Ranch.

Bryan first came to Idaho in 1897, the year after he lost his initial run at the presidency. During a post-election campaign stop at Shoshone, Bryan found himself on a stage coach headed to the Perrine Ranch, the site of the first farming activity in the area. The ranch was located in the canyon west of today's Perrine Memorial Bridge.

Bryan and Perrine became close friends, as did Hortense Perrine and Bryan's wife, Mary. Bryan spent the next decade on the campaign trail, running for office in 1900 and again in 1908. The Bryan family made numerous visits to Twin Falls during those years.

A lawyer by profession, Bryan opposed Clarence Darrow in the famous "Scopes Monkey Trial" in Tennessee in 1925, and died shortly afterward. Bryan is buried in Arlington National Cemetery. I.B. Perrine died in 1943 and is buried on his ranch in the Snake River canyon.

Over time, the rock monuments all but disappeared, as vandals tossed rock after rock into the canyon below. By the time Randy Perrine was in his mid-20s, only three of the six monuments were left standing.

In 1984, locals celebrated the 100-year anniversary of I.B. Perrine and his ranch – and as part of the celebration, Randy Perrine and the Jerome County Historical Society took steps to prevent further damage to the remaining monuments.

The monuments were secured with rebar and cemented in place. A fourth monument was erected, in honor of 100 years of farming in the Magic Valley, Randy said.

HIDDEN HISTORY

Despite the efforts to save the monuments, the rock towers have continued to disappear.

Just when the other three rock monuments in the Bisbee photograph were built remains a mystery to the Perrine family today.

"Who built the other three, and what did they represent?" Randy Perrine remarked that Monday. "That's my big question."

A photograph in a private album that once belonged to Jessie Bisbee, wife of Clarence BIsbee, has added more mystery to the rock towers.

Bisbee shot Bryan Point many times in his career, creating a partial timeline of the rock towers.

Bisbee moved to Twin Falls in 1906 at the urging of a school buddy from Nebraska, and brought his girlfriend, Jessie Robinson, to Twin Falls in 1910. Bisbee married Jessie in Salt Lake City.

But before Jessie agreed to marry him, Bisbee sent her scenic photographs from his new home. One of these is a photograph showing three rock towers on Bryan Point taken in 1906 — a full year before Bryan built the Perrine monuments.

While Bisbee's photo does not answer the question of who built the first three rock towers, it does tell where Bryan got the idea for the Perrine monuments.

The Bisbee photo album containing the 1906 photograph is on display at the Twin Falls County Historical Museum.

PHOTO COURTESY OF CLARENCE E. BISBEE, TWIN FALLS COUNTY HISTORICAL MUSEUM

Early Magic Valley photographer C.E. Bisbee's documentation of Bryan Point has helped answer some questions about when rock towers were built.

Mosler Safe at the Twin Falls County Courthouse

Just inside the Fourth Avenue entrance of the Twin Falls County Courthouse sits a Mosler "cannonball" safe, made in the early 1900s. True to its obligations, the only secret the safe reveals is that it once belonged to the Bank of Hansen. How the safe was moved to the courthouse — and better yet, why the safe was moved to the courthouse — remains a mystery.

The Bank of Hansen was opened in 1910 by Lawrence Hansen, a prominent farmer and justice of the peace, for whom — along with his brother John — the town of Hansen was named. The bank building was located on the northwest corner of Main and Overland in Hansen, and is now the Hansen City Hall.

The bank closed its doors in 1922, during an agricultural depression that hit

DREW NASH, TIMES-NEWS
An old Mosler safe sits at the Twin Falls County in Twin Falls. The Bank of Hansen was opened by Lawrence Hansen in 1910 and nobody seems to know how or when the safe showed up in Twin Falls.

HIDDEN HISTORY

this valley hard after World War I. By court order, depositors at the Bank of Hansen were paid a 15 percent dividend when the bank defaulted. Hansen had sold his interest in the bank a year and a half before the bank closed.

After the bank closed, Joe Froehlich Sr. of Hansen purchased the building in a sheriff's sale. The building then became the Hansen post office.

In 1975, Gary Kaufman was a young deputy working under Twin Falls County Sheriff Paul Corder. Kaufman, recently retired from the Idaho State Police, said he and other deputies were cleaning out a storage room on the main floor of the courthouse when they came across a large two-story vault hidden behind a storage cabinet.

"We moved the cabinet away from the wall, and found the vault door," Kaufman said. "Luckily, the vault door opened."

Inside the vault was the Mosler safe from the Hansen bank.

Kaufman said he was told by his boss that the safe had been taken during a bank robbery, and was later dumped by the thieves. It was hauled to the courthouse as evidence, where it has remained ever since.

No robbery of the Bank of Hansen showed up in a recent search of local newspaper archives, however.

The safe was brought out of hiding when the main floor of the courthouse was remodeled in the 1990s.

The Twin Falls County Commissioners have joked about donating the safe to the county museum, but "I don't know how we'd get it out there," said Commissioner George Urie.

"I'd like to know how they got it to the courthouse in the first place," Urie said.

The safe, which stands only four feet tall and weighs no less than one ton, will probably remain where it stands for some time to come.